CW01052522

Personification of Hope

Legacy of National African American
Political Leadership

Personification of Hope

Legacy of National African American Political Leadership

by

Daryl Lamar Andrews

Contents

Dedication

𝒯his book is dedicated to

My Wife, Tracy and my children
Donovan, Dorian and Tamryn Andrews

and

to the social and political consciousness and awareness
of the next generation of leaders.

Acknowledgements

"*You* can not possibly have a broader basis for government than that which includes all the people, with all their rights in their hands, and with an equal power to maintain their rights." No truer words could have been spoken from William Lloyd Garrison, abolitionist and staunch proponent for the equality of all people. These words still ring true today and it has fallen upon the present generation to ensure that history records the deeds accurately and document their reverberations. This task is a never-ending journey which requires counsel and direction from a number of different sources and it is with this in mind that I acknowledge the contributions of all individuals and organizations which have contributed to this work.

"He who finds a wife finds a good thing and obtains favor from the Lord."[i] My wife has been an inexhaustible supply of counsel and direction and her contributions were abundant. "A man of many companions may come to ruin, but there is a friend who sticks closer than a brother."[ii] Richard Berry, a fraternal brother and friend, helped to draw the linkages through the city and statewide ladder of the Illinois political machines. Brian L. Abrams, before his passing in 2008, provided direction on the contributions of African American Freemasons to society from the 1850s through the 20th century. These links served as valuable references which provided insight into the relationships that existed in the City of Chicago.

"My son, despise not the chastening of the LORD; neither be weary of his correction: For whom the LORD loveth he correcteth; even as a father the son in whom he delighteth."[iii] My father-in-law, Henry Turner, whose insight into several political figures provided correction on previous

---

i   Proverbs 18:22 - Holy Bible, RSV
ii Proverbs 18:24 - Holy Bible, RSV
iii Proverbs 3:11-12 – Holy Bible, KJV

assertions and direction to solidify these linkages. These helped to capture the true essence of a number of the political figures noted in this work. My parents, Clyde and Darlene Andrews, relatives and friends who lived through the eras in which many of the gains were accomplished. Their personal experiences corroborated many of the events of the day and age.

"For I was hungry and you gave me something to eat, I was thirsty and you gave me something to drink..." I remain thankful to the members of the Illinois Prince Hall Masons and the Phylaxis Society who also provide new points of reference at every turn. These points serve as a reminder to the roles of African American fraternal organizations in societal improvement from a historical perspective. Through relationships gained therein, many have been able to grow and contribute to the development of like minded individuals. This cycle has translated well historically into advances in the communities in which they live and serve.

"For we are God's fellow workers; you are God's field, God's building." My church family of Memorial Missionary Baptist Church continues to support each endeavor. Without God at the helm, where would I be?

Undoubtedly, these individuals and resources will be leveraged for future works as their insights continue to open new doors that beg for deeper digs. It is with their present contributions and future expectations that I acknowledge them at this time.

Introduction

$\mathcal{O}$n a crisp, cold Winter day in the month of January in the year of our Lord 2009, the hopes of millions of African Americans were realized in one swift motion. One man surrounded by family, friends and colleagues was escorted to the United States Capitol Building and was presented not only to an audience of thousands in attendance at the steps of the historic hall but also to millions through various forms of media across the globe. With skin of bronze and brows the color of midnight, he uttered the distinct words which had only been spoken by forty three other Americans before him. By the hands of the Chief Justice John G. Roberts Jr., he repeated those words with one hand raised and the other atop the Holy Bible that was owned, at one time, by the Great Emancipator, the Honorable President Abraham Lincoln. With solemnity of purpose, the Honorable Barack H. Obama took the oath of the Office of President of the United States of America as the first African American to hold the highest office of the land.

The inaugural moment rocked the foundation of the United States of America. For the first time in history, one, whose lineage was linked to the throngs of Slavery purely by virtue of his skin tone, reached a height that many have struggled to gain. Millions applauded and celebrated the occasion in person and in spirit as his selection fulfilled a portion of the hopes of generations past. It was the content of his character and not the color of his skin that destroyed the sum of all things relative to the walls of inferiority which were erected in prior generations.

Pushing forward despite great adversity is very familiar to the African American community as history outlines numerous examples of growth from troubled soil. This was certainly familiar to those who struggled to secure the rights and privileges inherent to all Americans. It was definitely familiar to those abolitionists who helped carry fugitives to freedom and very familiar to those who lived within the bounds of the Black Codes. Yes, the stage for Obama was laid by the efforts of a long line of predecessors who found ways to thrive in the troubled soil. Seeds planted in the 19th Century sprouted roots which gained nourishment from the battles for equality. The victories strengthened the roots which sparked the 20th Century growth that produced the tree from which Obama sprang. Without the former, the latter could not have existed. For a tree cannot grow without roots, branches cannot extend from nothingness and leaves cannot sprout from the mere air. Therefore, it is the achievement of the latter that qualifies the greatness of the initial acts. Tracing the acts through their various windings reveals that the tree from which Obama sprang grew from very strong roots and it is time to give them their just recognition.

The Local Roots
Chapter 1

"You will never win if you never begin"

- H. Rowland

$\mathcal{H}$ow does one determine the age of a tree? There are many methods but one form is to count the annual rings on a cross section of the stem nearest to the ground. Typically, each ring represents a year of growth and a careful study of each ring can help to determine the issues experienced by the tree within each respective year. A narrow ring indicates a struggle and a wide ring indicates favorable growth conditions. Therefore, these factors not only help to determine the age of the tree but also chronicle the trials that the tree has overcome to have survived to the present date. Two major factors determine the economic worth of trees include diameter and height. So, trees that are tall and wide are the most valuable because their strength allowed them to weather the storms of years past.[1] The source of their strength is a strong root system which provides the capability of growth despite the due seasons. As with politics and life in general, strong trees exist because they stand on a solid foundation which begs for a deeper understanding of their roots.

A view of the past reveals an extensive list of predecessors to the Honorable Barack H. Obama, President of the United States of America, who took extraordinary steps during their respective eras to secure civic and political power for the African American community in the State of Illinois. Of the locales, the City of Chicago contained some of the most outspoken leaders in the mid 1800s due to the increased traffic drawn to the city by commercial enterprise and

---

1   Illick, Joseph Simon. Pennsylvania Trees. W.S. Ray, State Printer, 1914, p. 32-33

Underground Railroad activity. During this era, abolitionists utilized the waterway and other methods to battle the Institution of Slavery whose throngs of degradation lived within this free state by virtue of the Blacks Codes which were instituted shortly after Illinois' charter in the year 1818. Through the efforts of John Jones, prominent Chicagoan and abolitionist, the fight against the Black Codes served as the start of African American political power in the State of Illinois.

A native of North Carolina, Jones first entered the State of Illinois through the City of Alton in the 1840s leveraging his tailoring skills and transforming them into a successful business.[2] Located at the convergence of the Illinois, Mississippi and Missouri Rivers, Alton was the largest city within Madison County of the State of Illinois during the early 19th century. A beehive of abolitionist activity, Alton was a major docking point for commercial traffic en route to Missouri, Central Illinois and Iowa and provided trade and employment opportunities for those who resided in the river cities. In addition, the construction of the Illinois and Michigan Canal, which had begun in the 1820s, shifted the residential dynamic northward along the Illinois River as many took advantage of the construction opportunities.

While in Alton, Jones had also become an active participant in the abolitionist movement through the Wood River Colored Baptist Association (WRCBA) and other abolitionist agencies. These organizations aided many fugitives to freedom in the north and it was

---

2   Guzman, Richard. Black Writing from Chicago: In the world, not of it?, SIU Press, 2006, p.3-8

through this linkage that Jones met his wife, Mary Richardson. The daughter of one of the founders of the WRCBA, namely H.H. Richardson, John and Mary both worked feverishly in the movement for freedom, equality and justice for the free and enslaved alike. Their zeal for the abolitionist movement was extended to the City of Chicago after their migration in 1845 and was sustained by the successful tailoring business of Jones. Their successes in both arenas placed them in prominent circles in the city and positioned John Jones perfectly for future success despite the civic and legal challenges presented during the day and age.[3]

With the opening of the Illinois and Michigan Canal in the 1840s, new opportunities had opened in the northern portion of Illinois. The canal, which was designed to link the Illinois River to the Des Plaines River, provided a clear path from the Mississippi River to Lake Michigan on the shore of the City of Chicago and drew commercial traffic northward to such a degree that Chicago had grown from a city of hundreds to a metropolis of nearly thirty thousand by 1850. These factors were the primary drivers for the migration of Jones and many others from Alton to Chicago during this period.

Although Illinois was admitted as a "free" state, African Americans did not receive equitable treatment under the law. The fact that these civic inequities had become legislated through the Illinois Black Laws threatened the security of African Americans within the borders of the state. Multiple iterations of the laws from the 1820s through the 1850s denied suffrage and limited the ability of

---

3   Andrews, Daryl. Masonic Abolitionists: Freemasonry and the Underground Railroad in Illinois. Andrews Press, 2010, p. 68-69

free African Americans to serve as faithful citizens within Illinois. For example, to enter Illinois as a free African American citizens, Jones was required by law to post a bond of $1,000 and apply for a certificate of freedom for himself and his wife to gain the privilege of traveling and living in the state per the 1829 law.[4] Prior laws instituted in 1822 subjected African Americans to be jailed and flogged if caught assembling in groups of three or more; forbade slaveholders from transporting slaves into the state for the express purpose of freeing them; and forbade free African Americans from testifying in a court of law or serving in the militia. Additions to the Black Laws in 1848 provided a means for the immediate nullification of contracts with Negroes or mulattoes who could not prove that they were allowed entry into Illinois, banned Negroes or mulattoes from holding public office and upheld segregation in free schools.[5] The very nature of these laws supported the assertion that free African Americans and fugitives were not welcome in the state. These laws resulted in the errand prosecution of many during this era and served as the backdrop for the rise of John Jones onto the civic and political scenes.

Through his constant challenges of the Illinois Black Laws, Jones had emerged as the unequivocal leader of the African American community in the battle to repeal them in the mid-1800s. By organizing the convention movement and coordinating with fraternal organizations, he secured the rights of African Americans under the

---

4   Andreas, Alfred Theodore. History of Chicago: From the Earliest Period to the Present Time: Volume 1. A.T. Andreas, 1884, p. 604
5   Eastman, Zebina. Black Code of Illinois. S.n., 1883, p. 44-49

law and promoted civic responsibility in all circles. He called a convention to order in 1848 in the hallowed halls of Quinn Chapel African Methodist Episcopal Church to develop a strategy to combat the 1848 iteration of the Black Laws. Though their efforts were unsuccessful, Jones organized additional conventions and private meetings to attack the issues through other channels. The civic efforts of the convention movement were done in conjunction with the abolitionist movement and helped to elevate the efforts of Jones and others in the African American communities to hero status. The other channels facilitated the Underground Railroad activities across the State of Illinois which brought Jones into contact with old colleagues such as Isaac H. Kelly of Alton, William Donnegan and the Reverend Henry Brown of Springfield. Their collaboration resulted in civic action in the cities of Alton, Quincy and Springfield which increased abolitionist activities to a high degree.

When conventions were called by Jones, representation by concerned citizens of color were often of an extraordinary size and resulted in action items which were designed to deal with the issues that impacted their respective communities. In response to the 1850 Federal Fugitive Slave Act, which further exacerbated race relations within Illinois, Jones called a convention at Quinn Chapel African Methodist Episcopal Church in Chicago to review the points of the act with a gathering of over five hundred colored citizens. The act escalated penalties for those who were caught aiding fugitive slaves and, in effect, deputized American citizens to help with the process of returning fugitives or those whom they deemed to be fugitives into the custody of federal marshals. The convention expressed the belief that the purpose of the act was to enslave every colored citizen within America due to the lack of provisions to guard against false claims. In response to the effort, the convention developed the Liberty Association to communicate the points of the act within the African American community. In order to and unify for protection against irregular and illegal usurpation, a colored police system was organized in Chicago to patrol for interlopers[6] While the abolition of the enslaved remained a high priority of the conventions, the federal act prompted further action from the convention which resulted in an Underground Railroad initiative to carry fugitive slaves from Quincy to Canada to freedom through Chicago. This effort sponsored by Jones, Charles V. Dyer, Henry Bradford and other Chicago abolitionists coordinated passage along the Illinois River and Illinois from Quincy to the Chicago through Alton, Quincy and Springfield contacts. Fugitives were directed from Alton to Quincy by the efforts of Kelly and carried by multiple train routes from Quincy to Quinn Chapel in Chicago. From Chicago, they were taken by cart through Northern Indiana to Southern Michigan and then to Detroit to cross over to Canada into freedom. Their joint effort resulted in the freedom of approximately ten carloads of fugitives to Canada to freedom.[7]

The success of the conventions and abolitionist activities were

---

6   Mann, Charles Wesley. The Chicago Common Council and the Fugitive Slave Law of 1850: An address read before the Chicago historical society at a special meeting held January 29, 1903.Chicago Historical Society, 1903, p. 68-69
7   Turner, Glennette Tilley. The Underground Railroad in Illinois. Newman Educational Publishing, 2001, p.24

communicated within multiple circles in the African American community. Many of the circles had national linkages and increased the status of Jones, Henry Bradford, Louis Isbell, Dyer and others in the Chicago area to higher heights in the 1850s and drew the attention of the African American Masonic Order known as Prince Hall Masons to the city. Richard Howell Gleaves, Representative of the Grand Lodge of Ohio and Deputy of the National Grand Lodge, established North Star Lodge in Illinois in 1851 with Henry Bradford, John Jones, Louis Isbell and other abolitionists as charter members. Through the relationship held with Jones, abolitionists represented the membership base of the two additional Lodges which were formed in 1856 and 1857. Griffin T. Watson Lodge was established in the City of Alton in 1856 under the leadership of Isaac H. Kelly and Central Lodge was established in 1857 in the City of Springfield.[8] This, in effect, secured a new line of communication through a social network which also opened the door to national resources.

The continuous pressure of Jones and his colleagues relative to unjust treatment under the law was unrelenting. The fight for the abolition of the Illinois Black Laws endured well through the Civil War and came to a zenith in the mid-1860s. In 1864, Jones and Chicago Tribune publisher Joseph Medill authored and published a 16 page pamphlet detailing the iterations of all of the Illinois Black Laws and denouncing every count. Jones used the pamphlet to increase pressure on state and national legislators to pass the Thirteenth Amendment to the United States Constitution to end Slavery. These

---

8   Andrews, Daryl. Masonic Abolitionists: Freemasonry and the Underground Railroad in Illinois. Andrews Press, 2010, p. 56-60

efforts led to discussions with Illinois Governor Richard Yates and Illinois State Assembly leaders which resulted in the repeal of the Illinois Black Laws by both houses in January of 1865 and prompted national Illinois officials to be the first to ratify the Thirteenth Amendment to the United States Constitution on February 1, 1865. The official bill for the state repeal was signed by the newly installed Governor of Illinois, Richard Oglesby, on February 7, 1865 and ratification of the Thirteenth Amendment was finally completed on December 6, 1865.[9] As the abolition of Slavery did not nullify Black Laws in all of the individual states of the Union and the former Confederate states, additional steps were needed at a federal level to protect African American citizens. Congress ratified the Fourteenth Amendment to the United States Constitution in 1868 which defined citizenship at the federal level in order to enforce the protection of a person's civil and political rights. This Amendment, effectively, combated the Black Laws in those states that continued to enforce them and provided a method for African Americans to leverage the federal courts for protection under the law.[10]

The national popularity of Jones had grown to an even greater stature following these legislative victories and carried over into social and political circles. He had risen in the ranks of the Masonic Order to the Office of Grand Master of the Grand Lodge of Ohio from 1865 to 1867 and presided over the formal establishment of a Masonic Grand Lodge for the State of Illinois in 1867 from the three

---

9   Andreas, Alfred Theodore. History of Chicago: From the Earliest Period to the Present Time: Volume 1. A.T. Andreas, 1884, p. 604
10   Wallenstein, Peter. Blue Laws and Black Codes: Conflict, Courts, and Change in Twentieth-century Virginia. University of Virginia Press, 2004, p. 167

Lodges which had been formed in the state. Three additional Masonic Lodges were chartered thereafter and further expansion prompted the brethren to name the seventh Lodge formed in the City of Chicago after John Jones himself in 1868. Riding the wave of success, Jones continued civil battles and helped to secure the ratification of the Fifteenth Amendment to the United States Constitution in 1870 which granted African Americans the right to vote. Subsequently, he was elected as the first African American to public office in the state as Cook County Commissioner in 1871.[11]

His election broke the color barrier within the state and served as the catalyst which galvanized African Americans in the political and fraternal ranks around issues that affected their communities. Of his most noted efforts as a Commissioner, he effectively dealt with inequities identified in the education of African American children. His efforts abolished segregation in the Cook County school system in 1874.[12] The legitimacy of the African American Masonic Order had also become a major topic in fraternal circles during the 1870s. The early expansion of Lodges across America were held to be illegitimate by some English and American Lodges as noted in an article published in the Chicago Tribune on January 9, 1876. Jones came to the forefront of the defense by issuing a series of articles which were published in the Chicago Daily Tribune to defend the negative assertions placed on the organization in 1876. With the assistance of Medill, Jones published "A Colored Mason's Defense of

---

11 Rather, Ernest R. Chicago Negro Almanac and Reference Book. Chicago Negro
    Almanac Pub. Co., 1972, p. 194-195
12 Ibid, p. 195

Prince Hall Lodge and Its Offspring" and "Further Defense of Colored Masonry" in January and February of 1876 to outline the history of Prince Hall Masonry in the United States of America and the legitimacy of its expansion through the same methods and procedures utilized by Masonic Lodges in Europe. An excerpt from "Further Defense of Colored Masonry" published in the Tribune on February 6, 1876 is the basis for the Jones defense:

> "The Lodge 'Minervs' also chartered by the Grand Lodge of London in 1741, has, in its turn instituted Lodges whilst still other Lodges of Saxony were called into existence by the Mother Lodge of the Three Globes. All these Lodges originating in the manner indicated were, and those which yet exist are, still recognized as regular Lodges. This practice is known to every student of Masonic history and every intelligent Mason knows this to be true that there has been no objection made and no complaint offered against this regulation by the Sons of Shem and Japhet until we, the Sons of Ham, adopted the same means (they having first set the example) to establish Masonry in this country among colored men."

This argument and the facts presented by Jones in the complete set of articles effectively ended the debate on paper but not the practice to deny recognition to African American Freemasons with linkage to Prince Hall across the globe. Despite the challenges, Prince Hall Affiliated Freemasonry endured and the battles of Jones in this arena further cemented his status as a man of courage, character, and means.

He was characterized as such unto death.

Often considered as the founder of the term "abolitionist", the famed abolitionist William Lloyd Garrison offered that "I am in earnest - I will not equivocate - I will not excuse - I will not retreat a single inch- and I will be heard" relative to the cause of the abolition of Slavery.[13] These words were echoed in the actions John Jones and serve as a reminder of the kinship which existed between those who shared a common cause at the risk of their own lives. John Jones died in May of 1879 and was mourned by thousands at his services held on May 23, 1879. Over seven hundred people including white citizens, fraternal organizations and civic and political leaders from across the country gathered at the home of Jones lining the streets dressed in full regalia and waiting in carriages which prevented the flow of traffic through the block of 43 Ray Avenue in Chicago. With an abundance of floral tributes, the services were conducted by Elder Raymond of the Second Baptist Church who commented on the life and works of the deceased in splendid form and lamented the loss of such an astute and dedicated man. By the strength of pall bearers Robert Warren, Richard M. Hancock, Joseph H. Hudlun, John Winslow, George Smith and Elijah Cleary, the body was taken to Graceland Cemetery in remarkable fashion under the lead of the rum corps of the Sixteenth Battalion Military Band followed by an army of Prince Hall Masons. Leading the Masonic contingent was John Jones Lodge #7 under the leadership of John J. Gross followed by the members of North Star Lodge, Knights Templar from Corinthian Commandery, the Summer

---

13 Douglass, Frederick, Brent Hayes Edwards. My Bondage and My Freedom. Spark Educational Publishing, 2005, p.342

Guards of St. Louis and the Brothers of Union Organization.[14] Such a show of respect had only been seen by those who witnessed the funeral services of President Abraham Lincoln nearly fourteen years earlier which serves as a testament to the efforts of Jones on behalf of humanity as a whole. The following day, William Lloyd Garrison died marking the end to an era which laid the foundation for future growth.

All in all, Jones' history as a Republican and convention leader created a loyal support base that was leveraged by those in his immediate circle. The influence that he cultivated was transferred to individuals in his circle of acquaintance by virtue of their kniship and friendship with Jones. It allowed for resource sharing and the ability to deliver votes representative of the African American community. In effect, these relationships formed a base, the Jones Base, that was leveraged by several to obtain election victories for prominent leaders of the African American community.

The direct support of Jones in 1876 led to the election of John W.E. Thomas as the first African American to the Illinois General Assembly. Thomas and Jones were both active members of Olivet Baptist Church of Chicago. A resident of the south side of Chicago, Thomas was a grocery store owner, lawyer and a real estate investor who received support from the black and white residents of the district through his relationship with Jones and his reputation through various business dealings. He was elected   Elected on November 7, 1876 to represent Chicago's Second District in the Illinois House of

---

14   Chicago Daily Tribune. "John Jones – The Funeral Services", May 24, 1879.

Representatives as the first African American Illinois State Representative and, to many, his election affirmed the equality and citizenship privileges marked by the repeal of the Black Laws due to the mixed support he received. Thomas utilized this influence to sponsor and obtain passage of the 1885 Civil Rights Act which prohibited discrimination in public places in the State of Illinois making Illinois the first state to enact such an act at the state level.[15]

George P. Ecton , who was supported by Thomas, was elected to the Illinois House of Representatives in 1887. A former slave, Ecton became involved in Chicago politics shortly after shifting residency from Kentucky to the city in 1873. His victory in 1887 was the first handoff in a long line of succession of African American Republicans that would enter the Illinois House of Representatives. He continued the battle for civil rights and succeeded in increasing penalties for those who abducted former slaves with the intent on returning them to their former states for prosecution.[16] He was succeeded by Edward H. Morris in 1891 who continued to introduce legislation to protect the African American community under the law.

Born during the era of Slavery in 1859, Morris, a Kentuckian, rose to become one of the most prolific attorneys in the City of Chicago. He was the fifth African American to be admitted to the Illinois BAR in 1879 and became a friend and colleague of Clarence Darrow, one of the most prolific attorneys of the day and age. By the mid-1880s, Morris had become known as the "Dean of Colored

---

15 Williams, Erma Brooks. Political Empowerment of Illinois' African-American State Lawmakers from 1877 to 2005. University Press of America, 2008, p.2
16 Reed, Christopher Robert. Black Chicago's First Century, Volume 1, Volume 1833-1900. University of Missouri Press, 2005, p.335

Lawyers" as he mentored many young attorneys through the ranks. After being elected to the Illinois General Assembly in 1891, Morris maintained his local roots through service as South Town Attorney in 1892. A founding member of the Illinois Equal Rights League, he leveraged his legal background to fight lynching and introduce legislation to protect teachers during his terms of service as Illinois State Representative. He lost re-election in 1893 but continued to serve as South Town Attorney and assistant attorney to Cook County until re-election to the General Assembly in 1903. During this term, Morris was elected Floor Leader of the House due to his vigorous personality and aggressive style of communication.[17]

In 1894, Theodore W. Jones, an avid businessman, followed the footsteps of his uncle, John Jones, in the social and political arenas. He and his family moved to Chicago from Hamilton, Ontario in 1856 via Ithaca, New York in search for a better life. The younger brother of John G. Jones, he was the first of the nephews to be elected to public office. He was elected Cook County Commissioner in 1894 due, in part, to his reputation as a successful businessman having made a fortune in the moving and furniture business. He continued to trend of supporting civic actions to benefit the African American community.[18] Through a collaboration with Dr. George C. Hall and other civic leaders, they formed the Civic League for the State of Illinois in 1897 to improve the state of the community by building a coalition to battle forces which saw to its demise. T.W. Jones also

---

17 Smith Jr., J. Clay and Thurgood Marshall. Emancipation: The Making of the Black
    Lawyer, 1844-1944. University of Pennsylvania Press, 1999, p. 371
18 Buckler, Helen. Daniel Hale Williams, Negro Surgeon. Pittman Pub. Corp., 1968, p. 69

supported the efforts of Booker T. Washington by serving on the Tuskegee Institute Executive Council. He would later serve as the founding president of the Chicago Branch of Washington's National Negro Business League (NNBL) in 1900. His civic efforts brought him into close company with many prominent citizens of the age including Charles S. Deneen, Cook County States Attorney. Through this relationship, T.W. Jones gained appointment for Ferdinand Barnett as the first African American Assistant Illinois States Attorney in 1896.[19]

The third African American admitted to the Illinois BAR in 1878, Barnett was born in Alabama in 1864. He was a mastermind who, after graduating from Northwestern University Law School, founded Chicago's first African American newspaper, *the Conservator*. Many of the Conservator's articles were written by Ida B. Wells who would later become the wife of Barnett. They focused with great detail on the condition of African Americans and racial issues which impacted that condition. By 1882, Ida B. Wells-Barnett gained editorial control over the paper which allowed Barnett to focus on law and politics. Barnett served as Assistant Illinois States Attorney from 1896 to 1910 having successfully litigating cases at all levels of the judicial system.[20] Through the support of Barnett, T.W. Jones, Morris and several others, J.G. Jones gained election to the Illinois House of Representatives in 1901.

John G. Jones was born September 18, 1849 in Ithaca, New York

---

19 Andrews, Daryl. Masonic Abolitionists: Freemasonry and the Underground Railroad in Illinois. Andrews Press, 2010, p. 91-93
20 Smith Jr., J. Clay and Thurgood Marshall. Emancipation: The Making of the Black Lawyer, 1844-1944. University of Pennsylvania Press, 1999, p. 370-371

and was the eighth African American admitted to the Illinois BAR in 1884.[21] Though controversial at times, he utilized his influences in the legal arena to aid in civic and political action. He fought against segregation on all levels including the fight against segregated hospital facilities at Provident Hospital in Chicago despite her mission to train African American nurses and doctors.[22] He felt that all discrimination, whether done by blacks or whites, was wrong and went to extensive lengths to express his points. He was a staunch opponent to the perceived accommodationist attitudes relative to race relations proposed by Booker T. Washington and supported by his brother, T.W. Jones, through the NNBL. These non-accommodationist attitude was also fully adopted by Barnett and Morris and served as the major factor which solidified their three-fold relationship in the early 1900s. To many, his ego and strong personality exceeded that of Morris which earned him the nickname "Indignation Jones".[23] However, his manner in accomplishing tasks was thorough and aided in the galvanization of Chicago's African American Republican contingents in the late 19th Century and carried over to the early 20th Century in social and political circles as well.

In the late 19th Century, Barnett, Morris and the Jones nephews, also followed the example of John Jones by becoming extremely active in fraternal circles. All had risen to high ranking offices either in the African American Masonic Lodges in Illinois or the African American Grand United Order of Odd Fellows (GUOOF). Barnett

---

21 Ibid, p. 370
22 Buckler, Helen. Daniel Hale Williams, Negro Surgeon. Pittman Pub. Corp., 1968, p. 71
23 Heise, Kenan. The Chicagoization of America, 1893-1917.Chicago Historical Bookworks, 1990, p. 156

was elected Grand Senior Warden of the Grand Lodge of Illinois in 1892 which ranked him as the third highest ranking officer of the Grand Lodge for the 1892-93 Masonic Year. He served in this role while maintaining ownership and control of the Conservator newspaper. Morris served as Grand Treasurer of the Grand Lodge in the 1880s while serving in various roles in the GUOOF. He was elected National Grand Master of the GUOOF in 1910 and served in this role through many of the race battles of the early 20th Century. J.G. Jones served as Grand Secretary of the Grand Lodge of Illinois from 1874 until his election as Deputy Grand Master, the second highest ranking office of the Grand Lodge, in 1876. T.W. Jones was elected Grand Lecturer of the Grand Lodge from 1878 to 1882 which ranked him as the seventh highest ranking officer of the Grand Lodge as the dean of instruction for the work of the Masonic Order.[24] These activities secured their popularity in many circles which elevated them amongst the highest rungs of the social ladder in the African American Community.

The social and civic bonds solidified the relationships between Thomas, Ecton, Morris, Barnett, the brothers Jones and other prominent local leaders. While differences did exist, they maintained a focus on civil rights and worked through the Republican Party to protect those rights through political channels as evidenced by their contributions during their respective terms of office. Their successes were leveraged to corral the African American vote at the turn of the 20th Century and build a viable voting bloc representative of the

---

24 Andrews, Daryl. Masonic Abolitionists: Freemasonry and the Underground Railroad in Illinois. Andrews Press, 2010, p. 89-91

African American population of the City of Chicago. The bloc, which represented 2% of Chicago's nearly 1.7 million citizens in 1900, had expanded by 68% by 1910.[25] This increase sourced from the migrants who entered the city from the Jim Crow south strengthened the bloc and created a force that virtually guaranteed votes for the candidates of their choice. It was from this base, that the succeeding leaders gained election and developed successors whose impacts were realized well through the middle of the 20th Century.

---

25 Reed, Toure F. Not Alms But Opportunity: The Urban League & The Politics of Racial Uplift, 1910-1950. UNC Press Books, 2008, p.28

The Maverick
Chapter 2

"When nothing is sure, everything is possible."

- M. Drabble

*B*orn on March 9, 1871 in Florence, Alabama, Oscar De Priest, the son of former slaves, was destined to become master and mentor to many. His father, Alexander, was a teamster who shifted the family from Alabama to Dayton, Ohio in 1878 to escape the lynchings and tyranny of the southern atmosphere. This environment provided new opportunities for the De Priest clan which allowed them to send Oscar to the Salina Normal School in Salina, Kansas to study bookkeeping during his teenage years. After school in Kansas, Oscar moved to Chicago, Illinois in 1889 where he became engaged in interior design and real estate management. The reward for his hard work and efforts in this arena was a bounty of financial dividends which would place him as one of Chicago's wealthiest African Americans.

By the early 1900s, De Priest had grown into a prominent investor, philanthropist and socialite. His success drew the attention of many not only within the 2nd and 3rd Wards of the City of Chicago but also within fraternal circles.[26] He had become a prominent Freemason in Oriental Lodge #68 of the Illinois Jurisdiction and utilized his notoriety within the real estate arena to gain entry into politics.

A Republican, De Priest was elected Cook County Commissioner in 1904 and 1906 following the leads of John Jones and Theodore Wellington Jones. As Commissioner, De Priest utilized his influence to build the Second Ward Republican organization and worked with

---

26 Ragsdale, Bruce A. and Joel D. Tresse. Black Americans in Congress, 1870-1989. DIANE Publishing, 1996, p. 35

Theodore Wellington Jones, Lloyd G. Wheeler, S. Laing Williams and other prominent businessmen in the City of Chicago to establish the Chicago Branch of Booker T. Washington's National Negro Business League.[27] Following his terms as a Commissioner, De Priest returned to the real estate arena and had amassed a fortune through various transactions. In 1915, he returned to the political arena as the first black Alderman of the Chicago City Council.

Alderman De Priest was an active advocate African American civil rights. He introduced a civil rights ordinance in 1916 to the Chicago City Council giving the mayor power to "revoke the license of any establishment that discriminated on the basis of race".[28] He also fought against discrimination in the employment of women and African Americans.[29] He lost re-election to this seat in 1917 and became more active in the business and civic arenas. As the loss was due in part to accusations of questionable dealings with unsavory figures and retribution against his civil rights actions, De Priest was indicted by a Grand Jury for conspiracy in allowing gambling houses, bribery and houses of ill fame to operate. However, by the defense of famed attorney Clarence Darrow and Edward H. Morris, he was cleared of the vice charges. Despite these setbacks, he maintained active relationships with all of his colleagues which led to further political promotion in succeeding years through the Chicago

27 Ingham, John N. and Lynne B. Feldman .African-American business leaders: a biographical dictionary. Greenwood Publishing Group, 1994, p. 200
28 Chicago Daily Tribune. "Negro Alderman Asks Law Forcing Society of Races". June 14, 1916
29 Gates, Henry Louis, Evelyn Brooks Higginbotham, and American Council of Learned Societies. Harlem Renaissance Lives from the African American National Biography. Oxford University Press US, 2009, p. 148

Republican Political Machine.[30]

From 1915 to 1923, the Mayor of the City of Chicago, namely, William "Big Bill" Thompson, recognized early within his first term the growing population of African Americans in the City of Chicago. He worked to build alliances with the African American community and forged a strong bond with De Priest. In doing so, he provided the backing from white Chicagoans in De Priest's 1915 run for Alderman in the Republican Primary.[31]

Support from the African American community, on the other hand, was split primarily between De Priest and Louis B. Anderson, floor leader for Thompson. Congressional Hearings on March 3, 1914 before the House Committee of the Judiciary spawned aggressive measures from the Women's Suffrage Movement across America. Chicagoans Mrs. Medill McCormick, National Chairman of the American Women's Suffrage Association (AWSA) and Antoinette Funk, AWSA Representative, spoke very strongly on the proposal to grant of full suffrage to women which stirred the fires of suffrage advocates across the nation. Mrs. Funk expounded "I see no reason why in addition to these you yourselves considering this subject – if there is nothing before you that meets your mind – should not initiate for yourselves something in the way of legislation to meet the demand of the women of the United States who are now clamoring and begging for political recognition."[32] The words and the sentiment

---

30 Tuttle, William M. Race Riot: Chicago in the Red Summer of 1919. University of Illinois Press, 1996, Page 195
31 Bukowski, Douglas. Big Bill Thompson, Chicago, and the Politics of Image. University of Illinois Press, 1998, p.49-51
32 United States. Congress. House. Committee on the Judiciary. Women suffrage: hearings on woman suffrage, March 3, 1914, p. 6

of her entire address carried great weight with those in attendance and translated into the voter turnout of the women in the Second Ward in the 1915 election. Female voters initially leaned toward Anderson. However, after considering the connections of De Priest within the political community and his active support for women's suffrage, the balance for women voters shifted to De Priest which played a critical role in the election results.

On February 15, 1915, De Priest won the Republican Primary for the Second Ward over Anderson by 562 votes. His victory placed him against three white candidates in the general election in the spring of 1915 namely Al Russell, Simon Gray and Samuel Block. The African American community voted in large numbers during this April election which, combined with the white vote, led to a victory for De Priest who received over 10,000 votes from the citizens of the Second Ward. Nearly 4,000 of the 10,000 votes were cast by women voters causing De Priest to publicly express the extension of suffrage to women immediately after election.[33] This victory further escalated the activity of Thompson's enemies who preferred the victory of the white candidate over De Priest.

In 1917, Thompson's regime was threatened by the Chicago City Council which approved investigations into matters of bribery, prostitution, and collusion with the mob. These investigations were successfully blocked by De Priest who was eventually linked to the same crimes of vice. It was by his silence during De Priest's trial that Thompson remained in the clear and solidified protection for De

33 Hendricks, Wanda A. Gender, Race, and Politics in the Midwest. Indiana University Press, 1998, p. 108-109

Priest. From these actions, Thompson was able to leverage the continued support of the African American Community in the mayoral election of 1919. Second Ward support had helped to gain his election to a second mayoral term.[34]

Thompson's victory was immediately succeeded by one of the most turbulent times in the history of the City of Chicago. In the spring and summer of 1919, murderous race riots erupted in twenty-two American cities and towns. Chicago experienced the worst of these riots when several black youths swimming near one of Lake Michigan's white beaches were attacked by bathers resulting in the death of Eugene Williams, an African-American boy. Five days of intense racial violence followed between white Athletic Clubs and black citizens across the city.[35] The first clash led to the injuries and beatings of twenty-seven black victims by the hands of the Ragen Colts and other athletic clubs across the south side of the city. Additional attacks over the remaining period were spawned by the athletic clubs themselves including those known as the "Hamburgers", "Aylwards" and others. These strikes were met by retaliatory strikes by groups of blacks citizens who were quickly arrested on questionable charges in many instances by the Chicago Police.[36] All in all, twenty-three black and fifteen white Chicagoans were found dead, more than five hundred others were found wounded, and thousands of black and white citizens were burned out

---

34 Bukowski, Douglas. Big Bill Thompson, Chicago, and the Politics of Image. University of Illinois Press, 1998, p.49-51
35 Chicago Daily Tribune. "A Crowd of Howling Negroes": The Chicago Daily Tribune Reports the Chicago Race Riot, 1919
36 Tuttle, William M. Race Riot: Chicago in the Red Summer of 1919. University of Illinois Press, 1996, p. 33

of their homes.[37]

It was during this period that the efforts of De Priest and others rose to the forefront. Attorney William J. Latham, founder of the first African American Insurance Company north of the Mason-Dixon Line - Underwriters Mutual Insurance, provided legal services to many African Americans free of charge arrested during the riots. He successfully litigated freedom for William Saunders before Judge George Kersten of the Criminal Court in the State of Illinois vs. Saunders – September 1919, William Tonson before Judge Joseph Sabath of the Criminal Court in the State of Illinois v. Tonson - October 1919, and several others who were arrested under questionable circumstances for weapons charges. Almost all were arrested for defending themselves in their own neighborhoods from white gangs who invaded with malicious intent.[38] De Priest aided the African American community by using his resources to purchase and deliver much-needed meat to the impacted communities. This effort removed the stain of the vice trial of De Priest allowing him to regain his popularity and renew his stature as a force in the African American political community.

In 1920, Thompson endorsed De Priest as one of the most prominent Republicans in Chicago which led to the selection of De Priest as a delegate to the 1920 Republican Convention.[39] The Great Migration of many southerners to the northern cities greatly increased

37 Chicago Daily Tribune. "A Crowd of Howling Negroes": The Chicago Daily Tribune Reports the Chicago Race Riot, 1919
38 Smith Jr., J. Clay and Thurgood Marshall. Emancipation: The Making of the Black Lawyer, 1844-1944. University of Pennsylvania Press, 1999, p. 296-297
39 Gates, Henry Louis and Evelyn Brooks Higginbotham. African American Lives. Oxford University Press US, 2004, p. 229-230

the population of African Americans in cities such as Chicago and Detroit. While their voting power, which was directed by De Priest, helped to secure the election of Charles Griffin to the Illinois General Assembly in 1918, the bloc had begun to lose support for Thompson as many who migrated maintained loyalty to the Democratic Party.[40] In addition, the sting of the Prohibition Era had a large impact on many elected officials which did not bode well during the respective election seasons from the perspectives of all voters. As such, Thompson lost election to a third consecutive term as Mayor of Chicago in 1923. De Priest, on the other hand, won election as Third Ward Committeeman in 1924 and, subsequently, used his resources to help Thompson's bid for reelection in 1927 as Mayor of Chicago.

Through the Thompson Political Machine, De Priest climbed the political ladder to higher heights. He gained appointment as Illinois Commerce Commissioner in 1927 and reclaimed his Third Ward Committeeman seat in 1928 with Thompson's support.[41] After one year in office, Thompson had successfully rebuilt his Republican Political Machine which flexed its muscle throughout the City of Chicago. In addition, he worked to obtain additional opportunities beyond the borders of the city leveraging De Priest as an ally. These efforts gave De Priest confidence in his abilities to play a larger role for the African American community and the Republican Party if elevated to national office. As such, the machine mobilized to win nomination for De Priest as the Republican Candidate for the First

---

40   Kranz, Rachel. African American Business Leaders and Entrepreneurs. Infobase
     Publishing, 2004, p.66
41   Gates, Henry Louis and Evelyn Brooks Higginbotham. African American Lives.
     Oxford University Press US, 2004, p. 229-230

Congressional District over challenger Chandler Owen, editor of the Chicago Bee. Through Thompson's backing, De Priest was slated as the better choice for the district which represented a growing population of African American voters due to waves of the Great Migration. He ran against Democratic opponent Harry Baker and won election as to the United States House of Representatives by nearly 3,000 votes in the fall of 1928. With this victory, he became the first African American United States Congressman from the State of Illinois.[42]

De Priest took his seat in Congress on April 15, 1929 as the lone African American and the first after a nearly thirty year drought. Immediately upon entering Congress in 1929, he and his wife became the targets of discriminatory practices which would serve as fuel for the succeeding battles. Jessie De Priest received an invitation to a tea hosted by First Lady Lou Hoover. The invitation caused a massive uproar from southern Representatives which prompted the State Legislature of Mississippi to admonish the Hoover administration to give "careful and thoughtful consideration to the necessity of the preservation of the racial integrity of the white race."[43] The publicity of the incident further cemented the support of the African American community behind De Priest and led to his iteration of a proposal given by George Henry White nearly thirty years prior. White, who was the lone African American in Congress nearly thirty years prior, fought for the reduction of the number of seats held by states which

---

42 Saunders, Doris E. 1944 Pre-Convention Maneuverings: The Day Dawson Saved America from a Racist President. Ebony, July 1972, p. 45
43 Carey, Charles W. African American Political Leaders. Infobase Publishing, 2004, p. 78

deprived black citizens of equal rights under the law. Though unsuccessful, White's statement was very bold for the time and met with much opposition as he was one of nearly four hundred forty members of the House of Representatives in the 56th United States Congress. The racial makeup of the House of Representatives during the 71st Congress was very similar, making De Priest's reiteration of White's statement even bolder and it is within this racially hostile environment that he remained steadfast.[44]

De Priest continued to promote socially liberal policies to the Committees on Enrolled Bills, Indian Affairs, Invalid Pensions and others on which he served.[45] The ideal of equality served as the fuel which drove De Priest to challenge inequity at all levels and to create new opportunities for African Americans as demanded by his constituency. Dr. John C. Ellis, Grand Master of Illinois Prince Hall Masons, expressed the frustrations cited by many within the organization and by the community at-large in his annual address to the Grand Lodge of Illinois on October 13, 1931:

> "We as a group in this country suffer more than any other group under present conditions. We suffer from disenfranchisement, color caste, discriminatory legislation in the law making bodies and are even denied the equal rights to earn a livelihood. It is no small wonder then that unscrupulous political propaganda should be directed to us as a fertile field of growth. As a group we have ever been

44 Martis, Kenneth C. The Historical Atlas of Political Parties in the United States Congress. New York: Macmillan Publishing Company, 1989
45 Ragsdale, Bruce A. and Joel D. Treese. Black Americans in Congress, 1870-1989. DIANE Publishing, 1996, p. 35-37

loyal to our country and I say to you that this loyalty is one of our claims to the right of a full citizenship."[46]

In response to this and other issues brought forward by his constituency, De Priest introduced a bill to offer a pension to ex-slave citizens above the age of 75 in the amount of $75/month to be distributed through the Veterans Administration. He called for Congress to make the birthday of the Great Emancipator, Abraham Lincoln, a national holiday. He fought to make the states and counties responsible for lynchings by holding elected officials accountable for lynchings under their watch. He succeeded in prohibiting racial discrimination in the Civilian Conservation Corps (CCC) during the Great Depression which was a source for many jobs during that era. He fought and succeeded in having an anti-discrimination rider attached to a $300 million unemployment relief and reforestation measure. He introduced a joint resolution authorizing federal courts to change the venue of cases if a defendants' rights to a fair trial was prejudiced by considerations of race, color or creed.[47]

The translation of these laws into action fell short in the enforcement arena during the 1930s. By 1933, lynchings had become the norm in the south. In response to a newspaper inquiry on a lynching in Emelle, Alabama in 1930, a white resident responded "What the hell are you newspaper men doing here?" asked a White man who had been part of the vigilante group. "We're just killing a few Negroes that we've waited too damn long about leaving for the

---

46 Most Worshipful Prince Hall Grand Lodge of Illinois. Proceedings. MWPHGL of Illinois, 1931
47 Ragsdale, Bruce A. and Joel D. Treese. Black Americans in Congress, 1870-1989. DIANE Publishing, 1996, p. 35-36

buzzards. That's not news!"[48] Though integrated by law, the CCC remained mostly segregated and lacked the appointment of African American leadership. Complaints, due to racial unrest and unfounded allegations, led to the disbanding of the integrated camps by 1935 which restored segregated units to the CCC.[49] Despite federal laws relative to the aforementioned examples, their lack of enforcement was evident and prompted civic action against the racially motivated customs and traditions of the day and age.

In 1931, De Priest appointed Benjamin O. Davis Jr. to attend West Point which sent shock waves through the military community. The first African American to be appointed, Davis started West Point in 1932 and experienced numerous tirades of racial oppression which appeared to be indoctrinated within the mindsets of cadets and leadership alike.[50] The Army War College produced a study in 1925 entitled "The Use of Negro Manpower in War". Per Davis "The study concluded that the intelligence of black people was decidedly inferior to that of white people, that blacks lacked courage, that they were superstitious, and were dominated by moral character weaknesses. It also stated that the 'social inequality' of blacks made the close association of whites and blacks in military organizations 'inimical to harmony and efficiency. The Army had approved this 'study' and used it as the basis for discrimination against blacks." The

---

48 Raper, A.F. The tragedy of lynching. Chapel Hill: University of North Carolina Press, 1933
49 Fechner, Robert. Robert Fechner to Thomas L. Griffith, 21 September 1935, "CCC Negro Selection" file, BOX 700, General Correspondence of the Director, Record Group 35, National Archives, College Park, Maryland.
50 Carhart, Tom. West Point Warriors: Profiles of Duty, Honor, and Country in Battle. Warner Books, 2002, p. 91

institutionalization of this inferiority complex led to Davis being ostracized by his classmates and additional efforts to drive him out of the institution.[51] Despite the challenges, the strong resolve of Davis to succeed served as the foundation for his endurance in the hostile environment.

Davis graduated in 1936 as a second lieutenant ranked 35th in a class of 276 cadets. Shortly, thereafter, he wed Agatha Scott on June 20th at Cadet Chapel at West Point and they made their way to Fort Benning, Georgia where Davis was set to report on September 12th. Their journey to Georgia found them eating in segregated facilities and this trend continued on the military base in Georgia. Although Davis was denied the same privileges as many of the officers, he remained steadfast in the performance of his duties and received high marks for his labors. [52] His resolve to exceed the standards placed on him and intelligence translated well into leadership in the succeeding years.

Davis was selected as the commanding officer of the famed Tuskegee Airmen in the 1940s during World War II and, under his leadership, men such as Daniel "Chappie" James and others would fight with vigor and honor and emerge as champions and leaders in their own rights. As a result of his stellar combat leadership and service, Davis would become the first African American General in the United States Air Force in 1954 and the second in the United States Armed Forces as James preceded him.[53] Davis' elevation

51 Ibid, p. 94-96
52 Earl, Sari. Benjamin O. Davis Jr.: Air Force General and Tuskegee Airmen Leader. ABDO, 2010, p.30-32
53 Homan, Lynn M. Black knights: the story of the Tuskegee Airmen. Pelican Publishing

continued and culminated in 1999 when President William Clinton elevated him to the grade of Four Star General and showered him with accolades. President Clinton stated "General Davis, you are the very embodiment of the principal that with firm diversity we can build stronger unity.....If we follow your example we will always be a leader for democracy, opportunity and peace. I am very, very proud of your service."[54] Davis' accomplishments and the success of James and the other African American Military leaders made a mockery of the 1925 study performed by the Army War College and their successes despite the odds produced a sense of great pride for the African American Community.

In addition to the initial appointment of Davis to West Point, De Priest challenged the segregated eating facilities in the House of Representatives. By virtue of election to Congress, all Congressman are entitled to the eating facilities of the House of Representatives. After defeating an attempt to denied him entry by Senator James Heflin of Alabama, De Priest introduced a resolution to end Jim Crow discrimination in the House Restaurant to the floor of Congress on January 23, 1934.[55] In his rebuttal, he declared "If we allow segregation and the denial of constitutional rights under the Dome of the Capitol, where in God's name will we get them?" He succeeded in bringing a measure to the floor to investigate the incident which resulted in a vote in favor of his resolution. Unfortunately, no

Company, 2001, p. 206
54 Jet. December 28, 1999. President Clinton Elevates Famed Air Force Lt. General Benjamin O. Davis, Jr. to the Grade of Four Star General. Johnson Publishing Company, 1999, p. 24-26
55 Carey, Charles W. African American Political Leaders. Infobase Publishing, 2004, p. 78

revisions were recommended to House Restaurant policies.[56]

While the views of De Priest were socially liberal, his views on economics were purely conservative as a Republican and led to a downturn in his popularity in the 1930s. He promoted a minimized role of government in the private economic affairs by favoring a reduced role federal regulation in the economy. He also opposed union empowerment and the bulk of the complex social programs proposed by Roosevelt's New Deal in the early 1930s. Though popular with many blue collar Americans at the end of the Great Depression, these initiatives threatened private enterprise and placed increased pressure on De Priest and others to thwart the proposals. Furthermore, an ongoing debate with Chandler Owen, whom he defeated in 1928 for the Republican nomination, had reached its apex due to personal and political differences in the planning and execution of "Negro Day" at the 1933 Chicago World's Fair. As the chairman of the National Negro Day Committee, Owen proposed admission to the event in Soldier Field which did not include entry into the fairgrounds. De Priest publicly opposed the effort as it appeared to segregate the affair from the main activities placing Negro Day "outside of the fair."[57] An avid newspaperman, Owen published his account in the Chicago Bee which had a negative impact on De Priest. As such, the editorial criticism by Owen and public opposition to Roosevelt's initiatives placed a bullseye target squarely on the back

---

56 Rudwick, Elliott M. Oscar De Priest and the Jim Crow Restaurant in the U. S. House of Representatives. The Journal of Negro Education, Vol. 35, No. 1 (Winter, 1966), pp. 77-82
57 Ganz, Cheryl. The 1933 Chicago World's Fair: Century of Progress. University of Illinois Press, 2008, p. 113

of De Priest in the 1934 election.

In his campaign against Democrat Arthur Mitchell in 1934, De Priest was flagged as a Hoover man who opposed relief measures for the average citizen and supported bailouts to white collar businessmen. Mitchell blasted these ideals to the African American community and leveraged the stances taken by the Republican Party during the Great Depression. Equal rights did not appear to be a Republican priority during this era and the assertion of a large influx of the Ku Klux Klan into her ranks did not bode well for the confidence of the African American community in the party. Furthermore, the influx of African American Democrats to Illinois from the South during the Great Migration shifted voting bloc further shifted loyalty from the Republican to the Democratic Party. As a result, De Priest lost re-election to Congress to Mitchell, an ardent New Deal supporter, due to the dissatisfaction of black Americans with the Republican agenda.[58] With victory at hand, Mitchell vowed to improve the state of the African American community through Roosevelt's initiative. He continued the same fight against discriminatory practices which started under De Priest as he also fought the segregated seating policy of the eating facilities at the House of Representatives and continued to push for equal rights under the law.

De Priest, the ardent Republican, mounted a failed campaign against Mitchell in 1936 but remained active in politics and business

---

58 Ragsdale, Bruce A. and Joel D. Treese. Black Americans in Congress, 1870-1989. DIANE Publishing, 1996, p. 35-36

until his death in 1951.[59] He would be avenged, though, by his mentee and fraternal brother, William L. Dawson. Dawson would become one of the most respected politicians from the State of Illinois at both the local and national levels.

All in all, De Priest remains as one of the most prominent African American politicians for the first half of the 20th Century because of his effort which showed a strong resolve through many dangers, toils and snares. His aura wreaked of a strong sense of racial pride and a spirit of sacrifice for those whom he represented. As the first African American from the North to hold a seat in United States Congress, his examples of success and endurance not only cemented his status as one of the greatest men in African American History but also one of her most humble servants. His achievements were extraordinary and it is from this stock that the starting point for the national line is sourced.

---

59   Ibid, p. 37

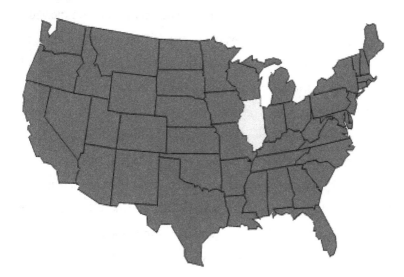

National Line
Chapter 3

"Individually, we are one drop. Together, we are an ocean." - R. Satoro

*$\mathcal{J}$*n the sport of Track and Field, the Mile Relay is typically the last race in most meets. In this relay, each participant is expected to run a quarter mile with a baton in hand. Upon completion of the circuit, the baton is passed to the next team member in line. While the participants in the relay change, the baton remains the same. If the baton is dropped by a participant during a circuit or is dropped during an exchange between team mates, the team is disqualified in most cases if the baton either bounces beyond the boundaries identified by the lane markings or if the baton is passed to a teammate beyond the designated passing zone. While the risk of failure is high, the reward is great which serves as the source for great excitement during this race that stresses teamwork, above all things, to reach the finish line.

A key to success in the Mile Relay is knowledge of one's teammates which can be obtained through practice, practice and more practice. This allows every member to gauge the strengths and weaknesses of a teammate and to improve upon the key components that ensure victory in the race. As individuals, teammates may engage different training methods which may cause one to be faster than the other. Practice helps one to better gauge the speed of the other which is an essential component to the relay race. Inaccurate gaging can result in the transfer of the baton outside of the transfer zone. Practice also helps to improve the probability of successful exchanges between teammates while in the transfer zone. Accurate synchronization between teammates is key. There are also other variables which are out of the control of the team that must be recognized and communicated during a race to allow room for adjustments. Inappropriate reaction to the variables can negatively impact execution. As such, support during the execution phases of the race not only helps one to avoid potholes but also elevates the confidence of the teammate. This helps to push a teammate to greater heights and to improve the overall performance of the team. These components work to build a knowledge base which can be leveraged to ensure that future exchanges of the baton occur at the optimal point in time, reduce the probability of errors and ensure that the most efficient race is executed on behalf of the team.

Relative to politics, the Republican and Democratic dogma have served separate training regiments for African American politicians. While many may have believed that switches between political parties of several politicians in the 20th Century represented grounds for disqualification from the races of the day and age, it can certainly be argued that the baton between African American politicians was never dropped because their focus remained primarily on the issue of equality for all citizens under the law. In lieu of the shifts which did occur, alliances still remained in tact and they were still leveraged to attack the issues. Overall, their ability to remain focused ensured that the baton not only remained within the due bounds for the African American community but was also handed to capable team mates who could carry it through the succeeding circuits.

Born in Albany, Georgia in 1886, William Levi Dawson,

developed into one of the most powerful politicians of the 20th Century. A member of Alpha Phi Alpha Fraternity, he graduated magna cum laude from Fisk University in Nashville, Tennessee in 1912 and studied law at Northwestern University in Illinois prior to his military service in World War I.[60] He earned the rank of Second Lieutenant with the 365th Regiment of the 92nd Infantry Division and, following the war, returned to Illinois in 1919 to complete his law studies.[61] He was admitted to the Illinois BAR later in 1919 and opened a law practice in the City of Chicago. A brilliant attorney, he became attracted to politics pledging his allegiance to the Republican party initially. In this role, he worked on various local issues under the regimes of Mayor Bill Thompson, Oscar De Priest and Louis B. Anderson. He along, with fellow soldier Corneal Davis played active roles in their campaigns and rose to prominence within their respective organizations. From 1930 to 1932, Dawson served as the State Central Committeeman of the Republican party and Davis played major coordination role in the Thompson Republican Machine.[62] It was through this relationship that Dawson had become a lieutenant in the national organization of De Priest and would reach higher heights in the political realm.

Both Dawson and Davis rose quickly by leveraging the same formula utilized by De Priest. Both had become active in the Prince

60 Beito, David T., Linda Royster Beito. Black maverick: T.R.M. Howard's fight for civil
    rights and economic power. University of Illinois Press, 2009, p.174
61 United States. 91st Congress, 2d session, 1970. Memorial services held in the House of
    Representatives and Senate of the United States, together with tributes presented in
    eulogy of William L. Dawson, late a Representative from Illinois. U.S. Govt. Print.
    Off., 1971, p.6
62 Bukowski, Douglas. Big Bill Thompson, Chicago, and the Politics of Image.
    University of Illinois Press, 1998, p.202-204

Hall Masons as members of Mt. Hebron Lodge and both had also increased activity in the Second and Third Wards of the City of Chicago. The relationships built therein helped them to become critical figures in the Republican Machine. Through the examples of De Priest and Anderson, Dawson and Davis parlayed themselves into greater positions of power and surpassed their mentors.

Dawson was elected as Alderman of the Second Ward in the City of Chicago in 1933 and served until his election to United States Congress in 1939. Both seats were formerly held by his mentor De Priest and, in these roles, he erected a new Democratic political machine. In doing so, he leveraged and worked to elevate his former secretary, William Harvey, to higher office. Harvey became Alderman of the Second Ward in 1943. He leveraged and worked to elevate his former top aide in the Second Ward, Christopher Wimbush. Wimbush had become the president of the Second Ward organization and was later elected Third Ward Committee by 1948.[63] Through Harvey, Wimbush and Davis, Dawson's power base was consolidated which allowed him to control the bulk of the African American voting bloc in Chicago.

Of his most noted accomplishments during his first five terms of office are the opposition of a poll tax which prevented Southern Blacks from voting and the defeat of the Winstead Amendment of 1951 which would have allowed segregation in the military after President Truman's desegregation of the Armed Forces in 1948. His intellect and quiet character had also earned him appointment as the

63 Grimshaw, William J. Bitter Fruit: Black Politics and the Chicago Machine, 1931-91. University of Chicago Press, 1993, p.79-80

chairman of the House Committee of Government Operations in 1949 which made him the first African American to preside over a regular Congressional Committee.[64] These accomplishments were extraordinary considering the lack of African American presence in the United States Congress.

Davis won election as Illinois State Representative in 1943 and would serve in that office through 1979.[65] In fraternal circles, Davis led the youth organization of the Prince Hall Masons of Illinois, namely, the Order of the Junior Craftsmen. While serving in this capacity he was a staunch advocate of civil rights which required much traveling on his part between Chicago, Springfield, Cairo and other areas across the country. In doing so, David ended discrimination against African Americans at the University of Illinois Medical School in the early 1940s, successfully fought against unequal pay to African American Teachers in Cairo and passed legislation which made it illegal to discriminate in employment within the State of Illinois.[66] These victories and many others gave Davis hero status in the African American community earning him praise and support on multiple levels.

Through the Democratic political machine, Dawson and Davis had amassed a powerful voting bloc which would be leveraged to place candidates of their choice into prominent offices. By the efforts of Dawson, Roosevelt won reelection over Governor Thomas Dewey

64 Hirsch, Arnold Richard. Making the second ghetto: race and housing in Chicago, 1940-1960. University of Chicago Press, 1998, p.129-130
65 Black, Timuel D. Bridges of Memory: Chicago's First Wave of Black Migration. Northwestern University Press, 2003, p.46-48
66 Andrews, Daryl. Masonic Abolitionists: Freemasonry and the Underground Railroad in Illinois. Andrews Press, 2010, p. 140-141

to the Presidency of the United States of America in 1944. Dawson is credited with delivering the Illinois vote. President Harry S. Truman leveraged Dawson and Davis in 1948 win election to the White House. They organized "Dollars for Truman" to raise funds for the 1948 reelection campaign which won Truman a narrow victory over Republican Governor Thomas Dewey and Dixiecrat Strom Thurmond.[67] It was also through the Chicago bloc of the Democratic machine that Martin H. Kennelly won reelection to the office of Mayor in the City of Chicago in 1951 and Richard J. Daley to the same office in 1955.[68] The contributions of Dawson, Davis and John Sengstacke in the Presidential election of 1960 were substantial. As a John F. Kennedy Campaign leader, Davis worked with Dawson to secure Democratic votes in the State of Illinois and on the Eastern Seaboard. Sengstacke utilized his publishing efforts to support the Kennedy agenda.[69] The efforts to organize and deliver votes in Illinois' First District on Kennedy's behalf were credited to Dawson and their collaborative efforts earned Kennedy victory over Richard M. Nixon as President of the United States in 1960.

While Dawson maintained a low social profile, Davis was well known in multiple circles. His activity in the Prince Hall Masons remained at a high level throughout his political career which gained his selections as Mason of the Year and Honorary Past Grand Master of the Grand Lodge of Illinois in 1979.[70] He was a proud member of

---

67 Ferrell, Robert H. Harry S. Truman: A Life. University of Missouri Press, 1996, p.296
68 Saunders, Doris E. 1944 Pre-Convention Maneuverings: The Day Dawson Saved America from a Racist President. Ebony, July 1972, p. 49
69 Travis, Dempsey. An autobiography of Black politics, Volume 1. Urban Research Institute, 1987, p.230
70 Most Worshipful Prince Hall Grand Lodge of Illinois. Proceedings. MWPHGL of

Omega Psi Phi Fraternity having joined the organization prior to his military service in World War I. Having been elevated to the rank of Sargent, he was a soldier of the highest caliber which served as a major influence into his style of leadership. He also served as a Deacon and, later, Associate Pastor of Quinn Chapel A.M.E. Church in Chicago and leaned heavily on his religious faith to carry him through rough times. His efforts in the Illinois State Legislature often brought him into contact with rising politicians with whom he worked to ensure the protection of the rights of African Americans in the respective ages.[71] As a mentor to many, he worked to ensure that those who followed were well equipped to handle the challenges of the future.

Dawson's primary focus was on the maintenance and extension of a strong political power base and his efforts easily identified him as one of the most prominent national politicians from the 1940s until his death on November 9, 1970.[72] His strength laid in his ability to build bridges across multiple boundaries and maintain strong relationships therein. With a focus on the future during his latter years, he supported and developed leaders in the same form as his mentor, De Priest did. These lessons were critical components to his success as they served the causes of his mentor well. In doing so, he passed the baton of national leadership to Ralph Metcalfe, a two-time Olympian who was known, at one point in time, as the "World's

---

Illinois, 1979
71 Jet. May 8, 1995. Corneal A. Davis, Civil Rights Leader, Former Illinois State Rep. Succumbs in Chicago at 94. Johnson Publishing Company, 1995, p. 18
72 Madigan, John. Radio Obituary for William L. Dawson, WBBM AM Radio, November 9-10, 1970

Fastest Human".

Metcalfe was born May 29, 1910 in Atlanta, Georgia. As a youth, Metcalfe's family moved to Chicago where he attended Tilden High School. After graduating in 1930, he attended Marquette University as a phenomenal student-athlete and excelled in both areas. A member of Alpha Phi Alpha Fraternity, he gained multiple nation Amateur Athletic Union (AAU) and NCAA Championship titles in the 100 and 200 Meter Dashes from 1932 to 1934, multiple medals at the 1932 Olympic Games in Los Angeles, California and the 1936 Olympic Games in Nazi Germany and graduated cum laude from Marquette University in 1936 as Class President. During his athletic career in track, he equaled or bettered more than ten world records and continued his education despite conflicts in the athletic arena. Metcalfe completed a Master's Degree in Physical Education at the University of Southern California and accepted a teaching and coaching position at Xavier University of New Orleans. He coached developed multiple, national champions in the sport of Track and Field until drafted to serve in the armed forces in World War II.[73]

After returning from the War, he returned to Chicago and became a civic force through efforts in the Chicago Democratic Machine as a lieutenant of friend and fraternal brother Congressman William Dawson. From 1946 to 1949, Metcalfe served as the Director of the Department of Civil Rights for the City of Chicago and was named to the Illinois State Athletic Commission in 1949. While serving in these roles, he also helped to solidify the Democratic vote of Chicago's

---

73 Hintz, Martin. *Wisconsin Sports Heroes.* Big Earth Publishing, 2002, p.66

Third Ward as assistant precinct captain which resulted in his election as Third Ward Committeeman in 1953. As the Committeeman controlled the city jobs of the ward, his influence had grown considerably which paved the way elevation. In 1955, he was elected alderman of the Third Ward under the new regime of Richard J. Daley, Mayor of Chicago and chairman of the Chicago Democratic Machine.[74]

While name recognition certainly was a factor in Metcalfe's election, he excelled in the political arena in the same form and fashion as he did on the athletic field. Through guidance from Dawson, he had become a close ally of Mayor Daley and quickly rose to the chairmanship of the Council's Building and Zoning Committee. In 1969, he was elected President Pro-Tempore of the Chicago City Council as the first African American to hold this position and worked through party lines to support the agenda of the Democratic Machine.[75] However, a racially motivated incident which occurred in 1969 would eventually force Metcalfe into a more independent role.

Founded in Oakland, California, by Bobby Seale and Huey P. Newton on October 15, 1966, the Black Panther Party was established as a means of local protection of African American neighborhoods from police brutality and evolved into a national organization designed to promote African American civic and political empowerment. By the design of Edward Hanrahan, the Chicago Branch of the party was raided by the Chicago Police Department in

---

74 Haskins, James. Distinguished African American Political and Governmental Leaders. Oryx Press, 1999, p.169
75 Ibid, p.169-170

1969 resulting in the death of well-known activist Fred Hampton.[76]
This event stirred the seeds of discontent in the African American
community and served as the blow which caused Metcalfe to shift
away from the Democratic Machine.

In the Congressional election of 1970, Metcalfe received support
from the African American community through Dawson and Davis
who not only controlled large voting blocs but also held membership
in the same Lodge of Illinois Prince Hall Masons, namely, Mt.
Hebron Lodge No. 29. Metcalfe mounted a successful campaign
winning election to the United States House of Representatives for
the First Congressional District but immediately exerted his
independence by refusing to support all of the objectives and
appointments promoted by the Democratic Machine.

The early 1970s saw Metcalfe publicly denounce police abuse in
the African American community and saw him refuse to support
Daley's choice of Edward Hanrahan for the post of Cook County
States Attorney in 1972. In response, Daley supported Metcalfe's
primary opponents in the subsequent primary elections for his
Congressional seat. Thus, creating a break which was never repaired
between he and Daley.[77] Despite the challenges, Metcalfe won
subsequent elections without issue.

Independent of the Chicago machine, Metcalfe continued to work
on behalf of his constituency at a national level to protect the rights of
African Americans under the law in a liberal fashion. In 1971, he was

76 Jet. December 10, 1990. Slain Panther Fred Hampton Honored By City of Chicago.
    Johnson Publishing Company, 1990, p. 9
77 Squires, Gregory. Chicago: Race, Class, and the Response to Urban Decline. Temple
    University Press, 1989, p.80-81

a founding member of the Congressional Black Caucus along with Shirley Chisholm and other prominent African American politicians. In 1972, he formed the "Concerned Citizens for Police Reform" committee to investigate police violence and introduced the Congressional resolution that officially established Black History Month. He was inducted into the United States Track and Field Hall of Fame (USATF) in 1975 and was named a member of the President's Commission on Olympic Sports supporting equitable treatment of all Americans in athletics. He championed multiple job and housing bills as well as access to health care for all citizens. He also played a critical role in the formulation of the treaty which returned control of the Panama Canal to the country.[78] These efforts mark his legacy and served as major cognitive factors for independent Democrats that would follow in later years.

Metcalfe's successor was Bennet McVey Stewart who was selected as the best candidate by the Democratic Committee without the consensus of the community to regain control for the Democratic Machine. Stewart, who entered the political arena in the City of Chicago in 1971 after being elected alderman of 21st Ward and Committeeman in 1972, received financial support from the Democratic Committee which earned him the nod in 1978. He defeated Republican challenger A.A. Rayner and earned a spot in the 96th Congress.[79]

Despite public disagreement with the selection and electoral

78 Haskins, James. Distinguished African American Political and Governmental Leaders. Oryx Press, 1999, p.169-170
79 Ragsdale, Bruce A. and Joel D. Treese. Black Americans in Congress, 1870-1989. DIANE Publishing, 1996, p.140

practices of the Democratic Committee, Stewart maintained a respectable level of support for the constituents of the First District. He leveraged his appointment to the Committee on Appropriations to protect jobs in the City of Chicago by supporting federal loan guarantees for Chrysler which protected employment for more than 1500 workers. He also supported federal emergency relief to provide low-income families with heating assistance and worked to extend the length of public service employment programs.[80] In 1980, he led the effort to investigate the Chicago Housing Authority (CHA) in response to complaints by residents. The analysis of the General Accounting Office revealed inefficient management of CHA resources and property. Though a machine loyalist, he carried on the efforts of Metcalfe to designate February as Black History Month stating on the floor of Congress that "we must not continue to permit the history and heritage of black people to be ignored.... If we educate our youth, black and white, about the heritage of our whole society we may be able to eliminate racial tensions that have existed in the past."[81]

Despite selection by the Committeemen for reelection in 1980, many in the Democratic Party did not agree with Stewart's initial selection in 1978. As such, the African American community rallied behind Illinois State Senator Harold Washington, an anti-machine candidate, who won the Democratic Primary by gaining more than

---

80 Jet. October 18, 1979. Fuel Stamps Proposed to Help Poor Keep Warm. Johnson Publishing Company, 1979, p. 7
81 United States. Congress. House. Committee on House Administration, United States. Congress. House. Office of History and Preservation. Black Americans in Congress, 1870-2007. Government Printing Office, 2008, p.504

50% of the vote. Following the loss, Stewart gained appointment as interim Director of the Chicago Department of Inter-Governmental Affairs from 1981 to 1983, served as Administrative Assistant to Chicago Mayor Jane Byrne during the same term and remained active in various political roles until his death in 1989.[82]

Born April 15, 1922, Harold Washington was born and raised in the City of Chicago. A graduate of Chicago's Du Sable High School, he was drafted into the armed forces in 1942 serving as a U.S. Air Force Engineer in the Pacific during World War II. Following the war, he returned to Chicago, attended Roosevelt University and graduated as the President of the Senior Class with a Bachelor of Arts Degree in Political Science in 1949. He, then, attended Northwestern University School of Law and graduated with a Juris Doctor Degree in 1952. After passing the BAR in 1953, he joined his father Roy Washington in the legal arena. Roy Washington, was a south side precinct captain with strong links to Democrats Arthur Mitchell, William Dawson, Corneal Davis and Ralph Metcalfe. While serving in this role in Chicago's Third Ward, he introduced his son to a multitude of African American politicians who provided Harold with expertise in the policies and practices of the Democratic Machine. Leveraging these experiences, Harold succeeded his father in 1954 as precinct captain which served as the starting point to his bright political future.[83]

---

82 Ragsdale, Bruce A. and Joel D. Treese. Black Americans in Congress, 1870-1989. DIANE Publishing, 1996, p. 164
83 United States. Congress. House. Committee on House Administration, United States. Congress. House. Office of History and Preservation. Black Americans in Congress, 1870-2007. Government Printing Office, 2008, p.524

A brilliant attorney, his initial political appointments fell within the legal arena. He served as Assistant Prosecutor of the City's Corporation Counsel Office from 1954 to 1958 and Arbitrator for the Illinois Industrial Commission from 1960 to 1963.[84] Through his stellar record of service in these offices, Washington was tapped by Metcalfe to organize a chapter of the Young Democrats of America (YDA) organization for the Third Ward to engage young adults in the political process. With Washington at the head, the organization had grown beyond the Third Ward by 1960 into a significant voting bloc of young African Americans with progressive ideas. Mayor Daley felt threatened by the power and ordered that the group be disbanded through Metcalfe. While Washington withdrew his leadership due to political considerations, he informally maintained his connection as an advisor to the group. His valued services in this role prompted the YDA of the Third Ward to approach Metcalfe to promote Washington to fill the State Representative seat left vacant by Kenneth Wilson who had been elected to the Cook County Board in 1964.[85] As such, by the endorsement of Metcalfe, he earned election as Illinois State Representative from 1965 to 1976. [86]

Despite his political advancement, he had grown frustrated with the Democratic Machine as he felt it tended to squash independent African American leadership. The first instance was the directive by

---

84 Alkalimat, Abdul, Doug Gills. Harold Washington and the Crisis of Black Power in Chicago: Mass Protest. Twenty-First Century Books and Publications, 1989, p.51
85 Green, Paul Michael, Melvin G. Holli. The Mayors: The Chicago Political Tradition. SIU Press, 2005, p.189-190
86 United States. Congress. House. Committee on House Administration, United States. Congress. House. Office of History and Preservation. Black Americans in Congress, 1870-2007. Government Printing Office, 2008, p.524

Mayor Daley which was carried to Washington by Metcalfe to disband the Third Ward YDA. The sentiment was further exhibited through the direct battles between he Mayor Daley in an incident regarding Renault Robinson, an African American Police officer. It was alleged that Robinson received unfair treatment by the police department because he was a founder of the African American Patrolman's League (AAPL). Washington initially supported Robinson's aim for the creation of a bill to create a civilian review board to investigate and monitor police brutality issues. As the bill posed a strong risk to Daley's police force, Daley mobilized the machine against it. Metcalfe, who had been protecting Washington's independent streak from Daley prior to the incident, was forced to withdraw his protection in conjunction with other prominent politicians that initially pledged their support. As a compromise, Washington served on the Chicago Crime Commission, a creation of Daley, to investigate the charges of unfair treatment by the AAPL. Unfortunately, the Chicago Crime Commission found the charges unwarranted.[87] This challenge to the machine prompted the attempted removal of Washington's name from the 1969 slate for the Illinois State House of Representatives. However, by the support of Cecil Partee, Illinois State Senator, and renewed support from Metcalfe, Washington's name remained and he won reelection.[88]

Washington's reputation as one of the most independent legislators in the Illinois State Congress was further cemented by his

---

87 Rivlin, Gary. Fire on the Prairie: Chicago's Harold Washington and the Politics of Race. New York: Henry Holt and Company, 1992, p.50-52
88 Hamlish Levinsohn, Florence. Harold Washington: A Political Biography. Chicago: Chicago Review Press, 1983, p. 100-106

fierce advocacy of African American rights arguably to a greater degree than did his predecessors. His challenges to a Democratic machine, which often shied away from racial issues to avoid polarization, were blatant and continued throughout his terms in the Illinois Statehouse. He maintained a strong focus on fair housing and employment for African Americans working to introduce a state Civil Rights Act that would align with the provisions of the federal Civil Rights Act of 1964. He introduced a bill after the 1968 assassination of Martin Luther King, Jr. to make his birthday a state holiday. The bill was finally enacted in 1973 with the help of Partee who had been elevated to the office of President of the Illinois State Senate.[89] He also introduced bills and resolutions to honor other civil rights figures such as James J. Reeb, Ralph Metcalfe and others who maintained a focus of equal rights for all under the law. While these efforts were in contradiction to machine stances, the tenacity he displayed and his stellar legal background led to his selection as chairman of the House Judiciary Committee in 1975.

Washington's efforts in the House were also recognized by many in the Senate. With the retirement of Partee from the Senate in 1976, Washington seemed to be the likely candidate to fill the void as he clearly stood out in the House. With the support of Partee, a strong campaign team which included Carol Moseley-Braun, and minimal support from the machine, Washington won election to the Illinois Senate in 1976.

89   United States. Congress. House. Committee on House Administration, United States. Congress. House. Office of History and Preservation. Black Americans in Congress, 1870-2007. Government Printing Office, 2008, p.526

The death of Daley on December 20, 1976 created a void in the leadership of the Chicago Democratic party. As Washington's frustrations with the machine were evident, he saw this as an opportunity to assume leadership of the machine which had caused him much turmoil during his terms in the Illinois House. As such, he mounted a campaign for the 1977 Chicago mayoral nomination but lost the Democratic nod as machine loyalist supported Michael Bilandic who eventually won the mayoral election.[90]

As an Illinois State Senator, Washington continued to align himself with a more liberal agenda as Metcalfe did at a national level prior to his death in 1978. In doing so, he was forced to reach across party lines and often defied machine leaders who worked to suppress legislation which focused on equal rights for African Americans. The Human Rights Act of 1970, for example, was drafted and pushed by Washington and others during the rewrite of Illinois Constitution in 1970 to restrict discrimination based on race and other factors. The Act, which was revisited by Republican James R. Thompson, Illinois Governor, after his 1978 reelection, risked the very fabric of the Democratic machine because the bill would limit the ability of party leaders to reward loyalists with political jobs and, thereby, decrease its power in the political ranks. In addition, since the bill was supported by the Republican Governor, the machine worked to crush it prompting them to publicly denounce the bill. Washington, however, worked between party lines in the Senate to gain passage of the bill on May 24, 1979 and leveraged Carol Moseley-Braun, who

---

90   Ibid, p.527

had been elected to the Illinois House of Representatives in 1978, to gain passage for the Act in the House on June 30, 1979.[91]

In 1979, Mayor Bilandic lost reelection to Jane Byrne, the first woman to serve as Mayor of the City of Chicago. Byrne gained entry into politics through the Daley regime after helping on the election campaign of John F. Kennedy in 1960. She served as Head of Consumer Affairs for the City of Chicago from 1968 until being fired by Bilandic after his election in 1977. She became very outspoken regarding her being relieved from the duties of her office and worked to mount a campaign to unseat Bilandic in the 1979 election. Perceived mismanagement of city resources during the Chicago Blizzard of 1979 produced negative press for Bilandic as the city had become paralyzed during the snowstorms.[92] As such, his inability to quickly end the paralysis painted him as being ineffective which boosted Byrne to victory.

The leadership and management style of Byrne has been classified as progressive as she appointed Charles Arthur Hayes as the first African American School Superintendent of Chicago and was the first to recognize the gay community.[93] She also brought extensive notoriety to housing issues in the Projects of the City of Chicago by moving into the Cabrini-Green Complex. Through these efforts, she gained support from liberals on the North Side of Chicago and the African American community. Unfortunately, these ideals strayed

---

91 Hamlish Levinsohn, Florence. Harold Washington: A Political Biography. Chicago: Chicago Review Press, 1983, p. 132-134
92 Fremon, David K. Chicago Politics, Ward by Ward. Indiana University Press, 1988, p.84
93 Costain, Anne N., Andrews S. McFarland. Social Movements and American Political Institutions. Rowman & Littlefield, 1998, p.64

from those of the machine loyalists which consisted largely of the old Daley guard.[94] As such, her reform initiatives did not receive a large degree of support and her candidates for elective office did not receive the support for which they had hoped.

After failing to mobilize the machine to support Edward Kennedy in the Democratic primary for President of the United States against Jimmy Carter in 1980, Byrne distanced herself from the old guard and worked to replace several in positions of power with new faces and block Daley loyalists. She successfully replaced George Dunne, Chairman of the Cook County Democratic Party, with Alderman Edward Vrdolyak but failed to block Richard M. Daley, son of the late Mayor, from the position of Cook County States Attorney in 1980. Daley defeated Byrne's choice, Alderman Ed Burke, in the Democratic primary and Republican challenger Bernard Carey in the general election.[95] Ultimately, these circumstances created a division within the machine which would lead to Byrne's downfall by the hands of Washington in succeeding years.

By 1980, Washington had successfully maneuvered himself into a position of power and popularity. With the machine in disarray by the hands of Byrne, he was able to increase his popularity in the African American community and cement himself as a powerhouse in the Illinois Legislature. As a result, his independent streak catapulted him to victory over Stewart in the Democratic primary for United States House of Representatives and a landslide victory over Republican

---

94 DiNitto, Diana M., Thomas R. Dye. Social Welfare: Politics and Public Policy. Prentice-Hall, 1987, p.249-250
95 Fremon, David K. Chicago Politics, Ward by Ward. Indiana University Press, 1988, p.78-79

opponent George Williams for the seat with over 95% of the vote. Sworn in on January 3, 1981, Washington received assignments on three favorable committees, namely, the Committees on Education and Labor, Judiciary, and Government Operations.[96] However, he refused to relinquish his seat in the Illinois State Senate as a protest to Byrne's attempt to replace him with Jim Taylor, an insider from her personal staff who Washington defeated in 1969. By doing so, he had hoped to shed light on the corruption of the Democratic machine and ensure that his replacement held similar beliefs. Despite Taylor's appointment by Byrne, he finally resigned from the Senate on January 21, 1981 stating "I was elected to Congress because the people are sick and tired of downtown bosses who want to handpick individuals to control our political lives."[97]

In the United States Congress, Washington continued the fight to eliminate discriminatory practices against the African Americans community and block efforts which would negatively impact his constituency without the backing of the Chicago Democratic machine. The latter placed him on guard during his early years which forced him to make frequent trips back and forth to Chicago during his Congressional term to maintain his solid base of support for the 1982 Congressional election. In doing so, he extended himself to great lengths both physically and politically which would pay the dividends for which he labored in the succeeding years.

---

96 Travis, Dempsey. "Harold": The Peoples Mayor: An Authorized Biography of Mayor Harold Washington. Urban Research Press, 1989, p.123
97 United States. Congress. House. Committee on House Administration, United States. Congress. House. Office of History and Preservation. Black Americans in Congress, 1870-2007. Government Printing Office, 2008, p.526

Washington assumed office at the same time as President Ronald Reagan who economic agenda proposed spending cuts for social programs which were utilized by Washington's Illinois constituency. Reduction in funding for college financial aid programs would have denied many of his constituents access to a college education. Washington and the Democratic National Committee also denounced the administration's budget and tax proposals which he felt would "balance the budget on the backs of the poor." Washington refused support of a proposal by the Education and Labor Committee to cut over ten billion dollars from student aid, employment training, and child nutrition programs during the 1981 budget reconciliation process.[98] He also disagreed with the increased production of nuclear weapons and military intervention in Central America as he the funds would be better suited for many of the aforementioned issues.

As a freshman Congressmen, he proved himself to be extremely capable by leveraging his personality and vast political experience to rise to prominence in swift fashion. In 1981, the Congressional Black Caucus (CBC) selected him as its floor manager for the extension of the Voting Rights Act of 1965 which outlawed discriminatory practices relative to African American suffrage. He successfully battled amendments proposed by Republican Congressman Henry Hyde which would have weakened the power of the act. After defeating the amendments, Congress passed the Voting Rights Act Extension in 1981. He also denounced proposals to weaken the enforcement of affirmative action and proposed endorsement of the

---

98 Ibid, p.526

Equal Rights Amendment (ERA).[99] Although the ERA was defeated, Washington remained at the forefront of the CBC and continued the fight for civil rights through his reelection campaign. With the support of the CBC and the First District of Illinois, he was successfully reelected to his Congressional seat in 1982.

After being approached by several in the African American community to return to Chicago and lead the Democratic Party, he announced his candidacy for Mayor of Chicago shortly after his reelection. However, the extension of endorsements to his opponents by high profile, Democratic leaders with national linkages presented a challenge. Senator Edward Kennedy endorsed Mayor Byrne whose support he leveraged in his run for President.[100] Vice President, Walter Mondale, endorsed Richard M. Daley.[101] Republican Challenger, Bernard Epton, was supported by Frank L. Rizzo, Mayor of Philadelphia who generated national attention based on his colored past as Philadelphia Police Commissioner. Rizzo's past showed a history of clashes with African Americans. As a Republican, he deliberately attacked the Reverend Jesse Jackson due his national status as an African American Civil Rights Leaders of the time in an attempt to galvanize the "white" vote in multiple cities against the vote of the African American.[102] As such, Washington was forced to embark upon a grass-roots campaign which bolstered his success in

---

99 Ibid, p.526-527
100 Barber, James David, Barbara Kellerman. Women Leaders in American Politics.
      Prentice-Hall, 1986, p.65
101 Morrison, Minion K.C. African Americans and Political Participation: A Reference
      Handbook. ABC-CLIO, 2003, p.230
102 Luconi, Stefano. From Paesani to White Ethnics: The Italian Experience in
      Philadelphia. SUNY Press, 2001, p.142

the civil rights arena and his anti-machine stance. With the support of Jackson's Operation PUSH, Voter campaign drives in the African American community during the period saw an increase of nearly 300,000 voters on the rolls which boosted Washington's confidence in his ability to win the office. In a competitive Democratic primary, he edged out Byrne and Daley and narrowly defeated Republican Bernard Epton to become Chicago's first African American Mayor.[103]

During his term in office as Mayor, Washington fought many battles with the Chicago City Council marking a period between 1983 and 1986 which has been deemed the Chicago City Council Wars. Although Washington won election as Mayor, approximately 60% of the City Council known as "The Eddies" were loyalists who did not agree with his independent stances of the past. Led by Edward Vrdolyak and Ed Burke, the bulk of Washington's proposals and appointments were voted down. The other 40% were pure Washington supporters and included former Black Panther Bobby Rush, Timothy Evans and Eugene Sawyer. Although Washington maintained mayoral veto powers, little legislation was passed but the battles which endured to obtain their passage were so sever that they earned Chicago the nickname "Beirut by the Lake". The wars ended in 1986 after a Federal court corrected the 1980 Ward Map which had unfairly dispersed African American and Hispanic voters.[104] The resulting special elections yielded four sets for Washington supporters which took the majority vote away from the Eddies and gave the

103 Fremon, David K. Chicago Politics, Ward by Ward. Indiana University Press, 1988, p.56
104 Ibid, p.132

Mayor the deciding vote.

Despite the challenges of the first three years, Washington remained active in social circles. He was a prominent spokesman at many affairs and supported the creation of the Chicago High School for Agricultural Sciences on Chicago's Southwest Side.[105] He joined the Illinois Prince Hall Masons and Shriners organizations and worked to improve benevolence in Chicago communities. These efforts won him reelection as Mayor in 1987 but, shortly thereafter, he died in November of that same year of a heart attack which produced a multitude of candidates to fill the void. With David Orr serving as interim Mayor, Aldermen Timothy Evans and Eugene Sawyer rose to the forefront as the two main candidates with Sawyer gaining the victory in 1988.[106]

The era of Harold Washington not only provided a solid base for future expansion but also produced a variety of capable African American political leaders who worked with the hope of abolishing transgressions against African American civil rights. Bobby Rush, Washington supporter during the Chicago City Council Wars, continued to rise through the political ranks after his election as Committeeman in 1984.[107] Carole Moseley-Braun, former floor leader for Washington, had risen to become the first African American and first woman to serve as Assistant Majority Leader in the Illinois Legislature in 1983. She also became the first African American and

---

105 Ibid, p.133
106 Kenney, David, Barbara L. Brown. Basic Illinois Government: A Systematic
    Explanation. SIU Press, 1993, p.148
107 Carey, Charles W. African American Political Leaders. Infobase Publishing, 2004,
    p.235-236

first woman to be elected Cook County Recorder of Deeds in 1987 through Washington's multi-ethnic, multi-racial, and gender-balanced "Dream Ticket".[108] Congressman Hayes, successor to Washington in the United States House of Representatives, fought for legislation to obtain federal funds to support vocational training and job placement programs within the school system. The author of the School Improvement Act of 1987, Hayes obtained millions of federal dollars to provide computers, textbooks and supplies for public schools across the country.[109] These efforts definitely helped to fulfill the needs of the African American community for the day and age but the dividends that they paid created a new, viable hope that an African American could hold the highest political office in the land.

---

108 Ibid, p.191-192
109 Ibid, p.130

Presidential Aspirations
Chapter 4

" *Great teamwork is the only way we create the*

breakthroughs that define our careers." *- P. Riley*

"*R*un Jesse Run!" chanted hundreds in the First African Methodist Episcopal Church in Los Angeles, California in August of 1983. In turn, Jesse Louis Jackson answered the chants accordingly with "There is a freedom train acoming but you got to be registered to ride. Get on board! Get on board!" He further articulated that "we can move from the slave ship to the championship...the guttermost to the uppermost...outhouse to the courthouse...the Statehouse to the White House" in answering the call to run for the Office of President of the United States of America in 1984.[110]

Jackson rose to prominence as a Lieutenant of the Reverend Dr. Martin Luther King Jr. in the 1960s through his service in the battle for African American Civil Rights during that era. After the death of King, he relocated to the City of Chicago to continue the fight which elevated his status amongst the African American community at both the local and national level. He leveraged this popularity to register voters during the 1984 mayoral election in the City of Chicago which gained Harold Washington the victory. Riding upon this wave of success, many called for him, a stalwart African American leader, to seek election for the highest office in the land. In response, he selected Mayor Richard Hatcher of Gary, Indiana to lead the Jesse Jackson Presidential Exploratory Committee to gauge support for this effort as a Democrat. The voter registration in the African American Community increased significantly with the prospect of Jackson

---

110 Time. August 22, 1983. Seeking Votes and Clout. Time Magazine, 1983, Cover Stories.

entering the race.[111] Unfortunately, Jackson fell short of the Democratic bid in 1984 and on his second attempt in 1988. Despite the losses, his spirit remained strong and he leveraged that strength and popularity to galvanize the African American vote locally and statewide. By these efforts he became the pulse of the Chicago African American community and the conscience of national politics. While Jackson's efforts were remarkable, he was not the first. He was preceded by five individuals who had gained prominence during their respective days - one, an abolitionist of the highest character who worked tirelessly on behalf of his people; the second, a minister who fought for civil rights in the 1960s; the third, a politician and socialist force from the City of Oakland, California; the fourth an ultra-talented African American woman from the South; and the fifth, a spirited African American woman from the East Coast whose tongue was as sharp as her wit. These individual are none other than Frederick Douglass, Reverend Channing Phillips, Ronald Dellums, Barbara Jordan and the fiery Shirley Chisholm.

Having escaped Slavery in 1838, Frederick Douglass gained prominence in social and political circles through the merits of his testimonials of life as a slave and self-emancipation. Working in conjunction with William Lloyd Garrison, Douglass began to speak on his experiences in the early 1840s to a broad range of audiences and his autobiography published in 1845, namely, "Narrative of the Life of Frederick Douglass, an American Slave" provided details on his story which inspired support for the movement to emancipate

---

111 Cheers, Michael. Richard Hatcher: Dean of Black Politics. Ebony, August 1984, p. 50-54

those who remained under the throngs of Slavery.[112] With editions of his autobiography reaching global destinations, he became a sought out speaker in America and overseas on human rights.

Douglass' success in his engagements prompted him to edit the "North Star" newspaper and other weekly and monthly publications to express his views.[113] In doing so, he also backed his words with actions by working with Chicagoan, John Jones, and other abolitionists in activities of the Underground Railroad and politicians to secure civil rights under the law. Douglass and Jones met with John Brown in Chicago on his route to raid Harper's Ferry in 1859 to discuss the effort and provide resources.[114] Throughout the American Civil War, Douglass remained as the conscience of President Abraham Lincoln relative to Slavery. His efforts prompted the Emancipation Proclamation of 1863. He was also tapped by Lincoln as a recruiter to build the 54th Massachusetts Regiment of the Union Army.[115] He, later, advocated the efforts of President Ulysses S. Grant to protect African Americans under the law following the end of Slavery in 1865. The 1871 Civil Rights Act was enacted under President Grant to provide a local remedy for abuses committed organizations such as the Ku Klux Klan against African Americans in conjunction with the Force Act of 1870 which made the intent to deprive voters, which included African Americans, of their civil rights federal offenses.[116] These efforts for civil and equal rights earned him

112 Holland, Frederic May. Frederick Douglass: the colored orator. Funk & Wagnalls Company, 1891, p.103
113 Ibid, p.149
114 Ibid, p.267
115 Ibid, p.308
116 Russo, Charles J. Encyclopedia of Education Law, Volume 1. SAGE, 2008, p.169-173

the label of the quintessential warrior for the disenfranchised.

While his focus remained on the improvement of the national African American community, he indirectly aided Womens Rights Activists during this period through his stances on equality. He had fought for equality for all citizens under the law which gained him much notoriety in the circles of women who also suffered under the law. As such, the Equal Rights Party took notice and felt that an alliance with Douglass would help to promote a political ticket which could implement change. In 1872, the party nominated Victoria Woodhull as their candidate for President of the United States of America with Douglass as her running mate.[117] Though nominated without his knowledge or consent, Douglass officially became the first African American to be selected as a candidate for the Office of Vice President of the United States of America with the selection by the party.

Abolitionist, author, publisher and warrior, Douglass remained a national advocate for equal rights which earned him selection as a United States Marshall in 1877 and appointment as Recorder of Deeds for the District of Columbia in 1881.[118] However, his most ambitious political selection was performed at the Republican National Convention (RNC) in Chicago, Illinois in 1888. He humbly addressed the convention reminding them of the sacrifices made by known and unknown African Americans for the ideal of freedom from invaders both local and foreign; reminding them of the blood shed by

---

117 Frank, Lisa Tendrich. Women in the American Civil War, Volume 2. ABC-CLIO, 2008, p.221
118 Turner Publishing Co. Retired U.S. Marshals Association Millennium History. Turner Publishing Company 2001, p.19

African Americans throughout the scourge of Slavery; and reminding them that despite the sacrifices that African Americans still did not have their fair share of protection of civil rights under the law. He asserted that "government that can give liberty in it constitution ought to have power to protect liberty in its administration" and urged for the support of legislation and action to enforce the rights of the disenfranchised under the law. His words stirred the souls who witnessed the speech and clung to every word of his rendition.[119] It stirred them so much so that he received one vote for the Republican nomination for the office of President of the United States of America.[120] It is this act which marks Douglass as the first African American to receive a vote for nomination by a major party for the office.

Contrary to Douglass' bid for presidential nomination, the efforts of his successors were more direct. In July of 1904, the National Negro Liberty Party (NNLP) formed and assembled themselves in a convention at the Douglass Hotel in St. Louis, Missouri. Their purpose was to build a national coalition to address voter registration prevention which was prevalent in the early 20th century across the country and other issues and concerns of the African American communities through the ballot. In order to accomplish the goal, the NNLP worked to select viable candidates for the Presidency of the United States of America under the direction of the founding chairman, Stanley P. Mitchell. After declining the nomination,

---

119 Republican Party National Convention. Official proceedings of the Republican
   National Convention: held at Chicago, June 3, 4, 5 and 6, 1884. C.W. Johnson, 1903,
   p.22
120 Ibid, p.177

Mitchell entertained the suggestions of representatives from 36 states who eventually nominated William T. Scott of East St. Louis, Illinois as a candidate for the Presidency and William C. Payne of Virginia for Vice President. Scott was a strong candidate who had gained prominence as the owner and editor of the first African American daily newspaper, the Cairo Gazette, and owner of a popular hotel and salloon. Having served as the third ranking officer in the Prince Hall Masonic Grand Lodge of Illinois in the late 1870s, he was also a member of the Order of Odd Fellows and other organizations which extended throughout all ranks of the African American community. His activities in these roles made him one of the most well-known men of color in the State of Illinois. He had become wealthy as the result of his ventures and, as a man of color, his status drew increased attention from the eyes of the law. Within weeks of his selection as a presidential candidate, he was convicted by local authorities for the management of a house of ill repute. As such, he was replaced on the ticket by George Edwin Taylor, a fellow Freemason, on July 20, 1904.[121] The Taylor-Payne ticket worked through the independent NNLP to promote the messages of equality and fight for the voting rights guaranteed by the 15th Amendment to the United States Constitution. While their message did reach communities across the country, they received scattering votes which did not present a substantial challenge to the major parties during the November 1904 Election. Ultimately, Republican Theodore Roosevelt won the

---

121 Walton, Hanes, Donald Richard Deskins, Sherman Puckett. Presidential Elections, 1789-2008: County, State, and National Mapping of Election Data. University of Michigan Press, 2010, p.277

election with more than 70% of the electoral vote.[122]

During the first quarter of the 20th Century, the African American vote supported the Republican Party in national and local elections. After all, the party gained election for Hiram Revels and Blanche Kelso Bruce as the first African Americans to the United States Congress in the 1870s. However, the diminished focus on African American issues led to a massive shift of the African American vote to the Democratic Party in the 1930s. As a result, many earned elevation through the Democratic Party ranks. Prior to 1940, there were no African American delegates to the Democratic National Convention (DNC). By 1964, the delegate count had grown to nearly 3% due to the loyalty in the voting record of African Americans for Democrats in national elections. By 1972, the delegate count had grown to 18% and the Democratic Party benefited greatly from the votes cast by nearly 88% of all African Americans for party candidates through that period.[123] With little deviation from the delegate counts and voter loyalty through 1989, it was within this ripe climate between 1968 and 1988 that the successors to Douglass, Scott and Taylor emerged.

In 1968, the City of Chicago was the scene of much turmoil under the leadership of Mayor Richard J. Daley, also the DNC Chairman, as racially motivated overtones and anti-war sentiment had seemed to set the stage for tumultuous behavior which occurred internally within the convention arena and externally across various points of

---

122 Facts on File, Inc. The World Almanac & Book of Facts. Newspaper Enterprise
    Association, 1907, p.268
123 Smith, Robert C. Encyclopedia of African-American Politics. Infobase Publishing,
    2003, p.115

the city. The death of the Reverend Dr. Martin Luther King Jr. which occurred early that year still wrestled heavily with the hearts and minds of many of the African Americans within the City of Chicago. The fervor and anguish carried from the riots which followed King's death were also carried in to the convention by city officials and delegates as there was a general fear that the convention would draw activists from all ranks into action on a national stage. In addition, anti-war activists such as the Youth International Party (Yippe) expressed their growing frustrations with the Vietnam War and stances on national policies through public demonstrations which were designed to demonize the powers at hand. As such, Mayor Daley increased the police presence to mitigate the perceived threats which met with multiple, physical altercations between the police and citizens of the city to which many attributed the violence to overzealous policemen. This behavior trickled into the convention through violence on its attendees. George Yumich, a convention attendee from Boston came face to face with a Chicago Policeman and left the meeting with a cracked skull. Campaign workers for Senator McCarthy who were also beaten in a similar fashion prompted Senator Ralph Yarborough of Texas to proclaim that the workers "were beaten with clubs in a political atrocity without parallel in American History." McCarthy later proclaimed that the police action was "completely out of proportion."[124] These acts in addition to the fact that the convention did not readily select Hubert Humphrey as the party nominee for President of the United States

---

124 Richardson, Darcy G. A Nation Divided: The 1968 Presidential Campaign. iUniverse, 2002, p.174-175

contributed to a tumultuous environment from which a viable African American candidate emerged.

Activist and minister, the Reverend Channing Phillips rose to the forefront as a viable African American presidential candidate in 1968 at the Chicago Democratic Convention. Phillips was born in Brooklyn, New York and migrated to Washington, D.C. in 1961 to pursue ministerial opportunities. He became the Pastor of Lincoln Temple UCC in Washington, D.C. and leveraged his success in the fight for civil rights in the South and political activism in the District of Columbia to improve the communities in which he lived and served. As the president of the Housing Development Corporation in D.C., he showed superior leadership skills and was selected as chairman of the delegation from the District of Columbia. As the chairman, he supported the campaign of Robert Kennedy until his untimely death in June of 1968. As a result, Phillips was elevated as the nominee for the office of the President of the United States in 1968 as Kennedy's replacement.[125]

While Phillips genuinely sought the nod from the Democratic Party, he utilized his newfound position to not only bring attention to the plight of the African American community but also iterate a vision of cooperation with minorities to build a party that would last. He cited the turmoil which existed during the 1968 convention as an example of this and felt that the inequities resulting form that type of mentality could be overcome. Although the convention ended with the selection of Hubert Humphrey as the Democratic Candidate,

---

125 Ibid, p.152-153

Phillips received a total of 68 votes placing fourth in a field of nine ahead of Governor Daniel Moore of North Carolina, Kennedy, Paul "Bear" Bryant, James Gray and Governor George Wallace of Alabama.[126] Like Douglass, the votes received constituted a symbolic victory and served as the foundation for the attempt at the office by another African American during the next election term.

A founding member of the 1969 Democratic Select Committee which later evolved into the Congressional Black Caucus (CBC) in 1971, Shirley Chisholm was the first African American woman elected to United States Congress as a representative for the State of New York in 1968. In the United States House of Representatives she served on the Education and Labor Committee and worked as a founding member of the CBC to promote the ideals of her constituency. A liberal at heart, she arose as a feminist leader during the early 1970s and promoted the ideal by hiring a staff consisting of mostly of women. Often labeled as the target of discriminatory practices, she maintained a streak of independence and fought tooth and nail on behalf of the poor and disenfranchised.[127] After frustration from the lack of support by her colleagues in many of her labors, she became convinced that her only recourse to invoke change was to target the highest office in the land. Against the wishes of the National Black Political Convention of 1972, Chisholm announced herself as a candidate for the United States Presidency that same year.

The Chisholm campaign was very active and her moves were very

126 Jet. September 12, 1968. Phillips Fourth In Dem. Presidential Polling. Johnson Publishing Company, 1968, p. 10
127 Persons, Georgia Anne, National Conference of Black Political Scientists. Race and Ethnicity in Comparative Perspective. Transaction Publishers, 1999, p.195

deliberate. She participated in the primary process and actively campaigned across the country throughout the fierce primary races against Humphrey and George McGovern for the nod in 1972. After hearing of the news of the shooting of Alabama Governor George Wallace whose public stances on racial segregation were renown, she paid him a visit in his hospital bed in an attempt to bridge the racial divide. She participated in public debates with the other candidates and extended herself through death threats to seek to nomination of the Democratic Party. Although, McGovern won the nomination in 1972, Chisholm earned a total of 152 delegate votes.[128] She summed her campaign up accordingly - "The United States was said not to be ready to elect a Catholic to the presidency when Al Smith ran in the 1920's but Smith's nomination may have helped pave the way for the successful campaign of John F. Kennedy in 1960. Who can tell? What I hope most is that now there will be others who will feel themselves as capable of running for high political offices as any wealthy, good-looking white male."[129]

While the Democratic Conventions of 1976 and 1980 did not contain an African American who sought the office of President, two did receive votes from the delegates out of respect for the duties within their respective terms of office. Barbara Jordan was best known for her role in the impeachment proceedings of President Richard Nixon during the Watergate Scandal Hearings in 1974. On August 25, 1974, clinging steadfastly to the Constitution of the

128 Smith, Robert C. Encyclopedia of African-American Politics. Infobase Publishing, 2003, p.64
129 Chapman, Ken and Anthony James. The Shoulders of Giants. iUniverse, 2005, p.26-27

United States of America, she outlined the causes for impeachment and was the face on the screens of televisions in the households of millions that officially called for the impeachment of President Nixon. He reputation skyrocketed as a result prompting the Democratic National Committee to tap her as the keynote speaker for the 1976 Convention. Her words stirred the hearts and souls of the delegates present to such an extent that she earned a single vote for the Democratic presidential nomination.[130]

Ronald V. Dellums of Oakland, California rose as a possible candidate in 1980 for the presidency based on his success in Congress as a Representative from the State of California. His efforts on behalf of the Congressional Black Caucus contributed to his stature as one of the most prominent African American politicians of the day and age. As many of his stances were sourced from socialist ideals, he drew strong opposition which also made him a polarizing force. Despite declining the nomination as an independent candidate for the presidential nomination in 1976 and 1980, he received three votes for the Democratic nomination at the 1980 convention.[131]

While the votes for Jordan and Dellums were purely symbolic, the attempt by their immediate successor, Jesse Louis Jackson, was deliberate. His failed attempt in 1984 which earned him a total of 466 delegate votes was also a victory of sorts as it gained him the support of the African American community at a national level and broadened his support base to include a larger range of nationalities. In doing so,

130 Wakhisi, Tsitsi. Barbara Jordan: A Legacy that Lives On. The Crisis, Feb-Mar 1996, p.4
131 Smith, Robert C. Encyclopedia of African-American Politics. Infobase Publishing, 2003, p.112

he leveraged diversity as a bridge to collaboration and utilized it to mount a second attempt at the presidency in 1988. In his speech to the 1988 Democratic Convention he iterated "...when I look out at this convention, I see the face of America: Red, Yellow, Brown, Black and White. We are all precious in God's sight – the real rainbow coalition." He further articulated the sense of legacy owing his opportunity to stand before the convention as a candidate to the efforts of Rosa Parks and the shoulders of other heroes on which he stood. He offered with a gigantic yawp "as a testament to the struggles of those who will come after; as a tribute to the endurance, the patience, the courage of our forefathers and mothers; as an assurance that their prayers are being answered, their work have not been in vain, and hope is eternal; tomorrow my name will go into the nomination for the Presidency of the United States of America."[132] With thunderous applause, the audience of the Democratic National Convention in the City of Atlanta, Georgia cheered the words of Reverend Jackson. With the speeches of all candidates and the votes of the delegations cast, the results of the polls on the centennial anniversary of the casting of a single delegate vote for Douglass yielded a victory for Governor Michael Dukakis of Massachusetts with a total of 2,877 votes, Jackson with a total of 1,219 votes, a host of others with votes of three or less.[133]

As the votes received by Jackson on that date marked the closest instance that an African American had come to receiving the

---

132 Lu, Xin-An and Rita Sullivan. Gems from the Top 100 Speeches: A Handy Source of Inspiration for Your Thoughts and Language. iUniverse, 2004, p.154
133 Kamarck, Elaine Ciulla. Primary Politics: How Presidential Candidates Have Shaped the Modern Nominating System. Brookings Institution Press, 2009, p.117-118

Democratic nod in the twentieth century, his status as a premier African American leader was further elevated on the national level as a result of his labors. His success in 1988 made him a natural candidate for the 1992 elections. By 1990, the Times Mirror survey noted that he had become the choice of 22% of a national sample Democrats and Democratic-leaning Independents for the 1992 presidential race ahead of New York Governor Mario Cuomo at 17%, President Jimmy Carter at 13%, Senator Richard Gephart at 10% and others.[134] In 1990, he had also extended himself internationally with the negotiation of the release of foreign nationals from Kuwait held by Saddam Hussein, leader of Iraq. However, personal matters had come to the forefront relative which cast a negative shadow on Jackson's campaign. In light of the reluctance of Arkansas Governor William Clinton to include Jackson as a running mate for the 1992 Democratic ticket, Jackson declined a third attempt at the presidency.[135] Instead, he focused his attention on galvanizing the African American vote behind candidates at the local, state and national levels who held their concerns at heart.

Of the candidates for the 1992 Democratic nod, Virginia Governor Douglass Wilder remained as the lone African American candidate for the office. A newly elected Governor, Wilder was the first African American to lead a Southern State in this capacity in the twentieth century. However, due to mounting criticism of his presidential aspirations in lieu of his state, he withdrew from the race

---

134 Jet. July 2, 1990. Jesse Jackson Leads in 1992 Democratic Party Presidential
  Sweepstakes. Johnson Publishing Company, 1990, p.4
135 Chapman, Roger. Culture Wars: An Encyclopedia of Issues, Viewpoints and Voices,
  Volume 1. M.E. Sharpe, 2009, p.282

in January of 1992 and his support shifted to Clinton.[136] With the African American vote, Clinton received 71% of the African American vote and, in the general election, he received a similarly massive percentage. In doing so, he defeated incumbent President George H.W. Bush and independent candidate Ross Perot and became the forty second President of the United States of America.[137]

While 1992 marked the lack of a single delegate vote for an African American Democratic or Republican candidate, it served as a testimonial to the true power of the African American vote. Clearly Wilder held the support of a large base and without it, the Honorable George H.W. Bush would likely have been elected to a second term. Other African American candidates who ran for national political office in 1992 also benefited from the power of the African American voting bloc. Chicago Alderman and former Vice-Chairman of the Black Panther Party, Bobby Rush won election as Illinois United States Representative. Per Clarence Page, "Bobby Rush went from being vice-chairman of the Illinois Black Panther Party to vice-chairman of the Illinois Democratic Party."[138] Ultimately, the results of the elections provided evidence that the African American vote was to be reckoned with and must be courted properly to ensure the future success of any politician despite his or her racial identity. This was evidenced by the lack of support provided to the lone African American candidate in the 1996 presidential election, namely, Dr.

136 Schantz, Harvey L. American Presidential Elections: Process, Policy and Political Change. SUNY Press, 1996, p.68-69
137 Mayer, William G. The Making of Presidential Candidates 2008. Rowman & Littlefield, 2008, p.130
138 Remnick, David. The Bridge: The Life and Rise of Barack Obama., Random House, Inc., 2010, p.313

Alan Keyes.

A true maverick who stood firm on his principles, Keyes was a political activist and diplomat who held strong conservative views which aligned him directly with the Republican Party. Although most African Americans maintained loyalty to the Democratic Party, the independent streak of Keyes drew great attention from the entire political spectrum due to his views on tax reform. Keyes offered "the 'soak the rich' tax proposals are therefore a politically shrewd way of getting the mass of our people to buy into socialist logic without having to declare socialist objectives. By following this approach, the day will come when our paychecks won't record our net pay; they'll record our government allowance." He further iterated "in words, it's a small difference, but in fact it's the difference between economic slavery and economic freedom."[139]

While he drew support from the African American conservative community through Black Americas Political Action Committee (BAMPAC) and other organizations, his views were unable to draw a sufficient amount of support from the African American community at large due to their conservative nature. As the support counts did not appear to be sufficient, he withdrew during the primaries. However, he did receive one vote at the 1996 Republican National Convention.[140] Keyes sought the nomination of the party again in the 2000 and drew praise from ultra-conservatives for his stance on homosexuality. He labeled it a "selfish hedonism" which drew strong

139 Keyes, Alan. Our Character, Our Future. Zondervan Publishing House, 1996, p.73-74
140 Business Week. A Jolly Payday at Solly edited by Larry Light. McGraw-Hill, 1996, Business week, Issues 3500-3503

challenges from the liberals and the gay community as a whole. While he exhibited great zeal in his efforts, he was unable to gain sufficient support to meet his presidential objectives. Despite the challenges he earned 23 votes in 2000 behind Governor George W. Bush of Texas who later defeated Vice President Al Gore for the presidency.[141] In 2004, Keyes focused on the Illinois State Senate seat because a Republican was already seated in the White House but two candidates arose from the Democratic Party to secure the presence of an African American in the primary races – Reverend Al Sharpton and Senator Carole Moseley-Braun.

In August of 2001 Reverend Al Sharpton announced his intent to form a presidential exploratory committee for the 2004 presidential election. Minister, civil rights activist, and radio talk show host, Sharpton was renown for his diligence in confronting injustice in all shapes and forms through the National Action Network and turned to Harvard professor Cornel West in 2001 to lead the unofficial exploratory committee efforts. This combination led to an extensive voter registration movement by the National Action Network which extended through 2003. After a review of the findings and voter registration totals, Sharpton formally established an official exploratory committee and pushed forward as a candidate for the presidency.[142]

A seasoned politician, Carole Moseley-Braun first rose from the Chicago Harold Washington era to a prominent role in the Illinois

---

141 Chapman, Roger. Culture Wars: An Encyclopedia of Issues, Viewpoints and Voices, Volume 1. M.E. Sharpe, 2009, p.298
142 Cowan, Rosemary. Cornel West: The Politics of Redemption. Wiley-Blackwell, 2003, p.155

State legislature. Her labors on the state level were well respected and led to her further elevation to national prominence with her victory over Senator Alan Dixon as the first African American woman elected to the United States Senate.[143] As the lone African American in the Senate, she served on the Committees of Banking and Housing and Urban Affairs and leveraged her colleagues to take strong stances against multiples issues. She fought the federal patent of the symbol of the United Daughters of the Confederacy stating that the Confederate Flag "has no place in modern times, no place in this body, and no place in society. I would like to put a stake through the heart of this Dracula." This led to the rejection of the patent.[144] She was a strong pro-choice advocate who voted against the ban on partial-birth abortions but voted for the death penalty and gun control. Contrary to the majority of the Senate and many of her Democratic colleagues, she voted against two high profile acts. The Communications Decency Act which was supported by President Clinton was designed to prohibit indecent material to children across the Internet She voted against it and it was later struck down by the Supreme Court in 1997 due to its vagueness and potential to abridge rights designated by the First Amendment of the United States Constitution.[145] The Defense of Marriage Act of 1996 was an attempt to shift the issuance of marriage licenses from the state to the federal level. She voted against the bill citing that "It (issuing marriage

---

143 D'Orio, Wayne. Carol Moseley-Braun. Infobase Publishing, 2004, p.35
144 Brill-Scheuer, Alida and Alida Brill. A Rising Public Voice: Women in Politics
  Worldwide. Feminist Press, 1995, p.134
145 Hartman, Gary R., Roy M. Mersky, Cindy L. Tate, United States Supreme Court.
  Landmark Supreme Court Cases: The Most Influential Decisions of the Supreme Court
  of the United States. Infobase Publishing, 2004, p.421

licenses) is not something the Federal Government does. Yet, in this instance, the so-called Defense of Marriage Act, we are moving into the marriage business unilaterally in order to prohibit the approval by one State of another State's decision to recognize a particular marital or domestic arrangement."[146] Her strong stances were clearly anti-conservative in many instances which, in addition to her independence, made her a prime target of the Republican party. In the 1998, the Republican Party successfully ran millionaire Peter Fitzgerald against her for the United States Senate seat winning a very close race by a margin of nearly 3%. After a brief retirement, she gained appointed as United States Ambassador to New Zealand by President Clinton in 1999 and served in this role through 2001.[147] She later emerged as a candidate for the presidency formally announcing her intention to run for the office in February of 2003.[148]

While Sharpton and Moseley-Braun fought vigorously against a field of candidates to obtain the nod of the Democratic Party for the presidency, their efforts fell short. Both shined during the Presidential Debates of the Congressional Black Caucus in 2003 as they relentlessly hammered the intrusive policies of President George W. Bush relative to the Patriot Act.[149] With the endorsements of Senator Paul M. Simon, Representatives Danny Davis and Bobby Rush, Moseley-Braun leveraged her record as a United States Senator and stellar service in all of the elective and appointive offices held.

146 U.S. Congress, Senate 1996b, SI0I04
147 D'Orio, Wayne. Carol Moseley-Braun. Infobase Publishing, 2004, p.90
148 Ibid, p.96
149 Jet, September 29, 2003. Moseley-Braun and Sharpton Take Spotlight at Black Caucus' Presidential Debate. Johnson Publishing Company, 2003, p.4

However, in light of her standings in the political polls, she withdrew from the race prior to the Iowa Caucuses and granted her support to the initial front-runner, Vermont Governor Howard Dean.[150] Sharpton, on the other hand, remained in the contest but was unable to gain ground despite respectable showings in the nationally televised debates. As such, he withdrew during the primaries and announced his support for Senator John Kerry.[151] Moseley-Braun, later, shifted her support at the Democratic Convention. With their support and electrifying speeches from Jesse Jackson Sr., Sharpton, Moseley-Braun, Representative Charles Rangel and a host of other prominent African American civic and political leaders, the 2004 Democratic National Convention revealed Kerry as the Democratic nominee with over 2,500 delegate votes followed by John Edwards, Dean, General Wesley Clark, Dennis Kucinich and Sharpton.[152]

Although the votes received by Sharpton were largely symbolic, the power and presence of the African American vote was seen by Kerry as a critical force in the general election. In response, he launched a two million dollar campaign directed at the African American community. While the initial advertisements included Kerry hugging and intermingling with African American voters, the substance of the advertisements relative to the African American community appeared to be lacking per the Congressional Black Caucus who felt that the ads would not resonate well with the intended audience. He later, added several highly respected African

150 D'Orio, Wayne. Carol Moseley-Braun. Infobase Publishing, 2004, p.96
151 Jet, April 5, 2004. National Report. Johnson Publishing Company, 2004, p.8
152 Janda, Kenneth, Jeffrey M. Berry, Jerry Goldman. The Challenge of Democracy 2008 Update: Government in America. Cengage Learning, 2007, p.272

American strategists to his campaign team to advise him on advertisements, debates, domestic policy and voter turnout. With their advisement, Kerry's initial vagueness relative to the issues and concerns of the African American community were clarified and he shifted his points of focus and style of speaking to become more engaging. In doing so, he focused on the rate of high unemployment and business opportunities in the African American communities and even courted his audiences with scripture in the same form and fashion as a baptist preacher. He provided details on community development initiatives to tackle the aforementioned issues[153] These changes helped to transform his image into a candidate who was truly ready, willing and able to work on their behalf. Despite the transformation and receipt of 88% of the African American vote, he still lacked the support of voters from the South who remained loyal to the incumbent. In 2004, President George W. Bush defeated Kerry by the count of 286 electoral votes to 252.[154-155]

Overall, the power of the African American vote was a major influence in the presidential elections of the late 20th and early 21st centuries. While African American candidates have had a consistent presence in the presidential races during these periods, chances of success in the contests for the highest office of the land remained low due to the lack of support by a broad coalition. As such, the true hope

---

153 America's Future. The Crisis, Sep-Oct 2004, p.23
154 Survey by Edison Media Research/Mitofsky International for the National Election Pool (ABC News, Associated Press, CBS News, CNN, Fox News, NBC News). Sample of 13, 719 voters consisted of 11,7190 voters as they left the voting booths on Election Day November 2, 2004 and a telephone absentee/early voters survey of 2000 respondents conducted October 25-31, 2004
155 McMahon, Kevin J., David M. Rankin, Donald W. Beachler. Winning the White House, 2008. Macmillan, 2009, p.109

of millions to, one day, transform presidential aspiration into actuality elevated with each iteration. With sights set for the 2008 election seasons, millions continued to yearn for that hope to become a reality in a definitive way. Unbeknown to many, the product of hope was already revealed in the form of the keynote speaker of the 2004 Democratic National Convention - Senator Barack H. Obama.

Hope Personified
Chapter 5

"Never let go of hope. One day you will see that it all has finally come together." - Anonymous

"*Now* faith is the substance of things hoped for, the evidence of things not seen."[156] These words were written by the Apostle Paul in one of his many letters to the church and they inspired the followers of Christ to continue their labors despite the challenges that were presented before them in that day and age. It was that faith, that unshakable belief that extended the church across the globe. It was also that same faith which sustained the ancestors of African American descent through the trials of Slavery and beyond. It was certainly that same unshakable faith shared by Frederick Douglass in the hopes and dreams of a colorless America in which anyone, despite their racial demographic, could achieve the desires of one's heart. For by that faith, six score years after the receipt of a single presidential delegate vote for an African American, was the hope of an African American President of the United States finally substantiated.

The Honorable Barack H. Obama Jr. was born in Honolulu, Hawaii on August 4, 1961 to the union of Barack Obama Sr. and Stanley Ann Dunham. The marital union was short-lived as his parents divorced in 1964 but his mother, later, remarried in 1967 and moved the family to Indonesia. In 1971, Obama moved back to Hawaii to live with his maternal Grandparents where he continued his education. He graduated from Punahou School in 1979 and, shortly thereafter, moved to Los Angeles, California and attended Occidental College where he first became active in socio-political activities on a

---

156 Hebrews 11:1 – Holy Bible, KJV

large scale. In 1981 he called for Occidental's divestment from South Africa in protest to her system of Apartheid or legal segregation based on race. He later transferred to Columbia University in New York in 1981 to better channel these energies. He graduated with a Bachelor of Arts Degree in Political Science with a specialty in International Relations from Columbia in 1983.[157] He, then, parlayed his skill set into employment with the Business International Corporation (BIC) and the New York Public Interest Research Group (NYPIRC).[158] His roles in these companies presented him with access to the international business community and the national political arena.

The election of Harold Washington as the first African American Mayor of the City of Chicago inspired Obama to shift his residence to the Windy City. He admired the fact that Washington had won election in 1983 despite separating himself from the Chicago Democratic Machine like his predecessor, Ralph Metcalfe. Washington he felt that the Machine did not have the best interests of the African American community at heart and worked through independent channels to meet his political objectives.

Working with Jesse Jackson and others, the Southside Voter Registration drive registered a substantial number of African American voters during the 1983 mayoral campaign whose votes were the critical factor for Washington's victory in the Democratic Primary over two white candidates, namely, incumbent Mayor Jane Byrne and Richard M. Daley. As a result, racial tensions in the city

157 Edgar, Thorpe. The Pearson Current Events Digest 2009. Pearson Education India, 2009, p.68
158 Remnick, David. The Bridge: The Life and rise of Barack Obama, Random House, 2010, p.118-121

increased ten fold and this was revealed during the general election against Republican Bernard Epton with greater ferver. Washington was often attacked along racial lines at campaign stops often being greeted with the words "Die, Nigger, Die" under showers of rocks.[159] Despite the challenges, his victory over Epton sent shock waves which reverberated across the country and they drew the attention of the nation to the Midwest.

Inspired by the victory, Obama applied for a job in the Washington administration and moved to Chicago without confirmation of employment. Upon arrival, he focused on becoming positive influence in the Chicago area and built upon that basis. In doing so, he became a civic and political giant within the communities in which he served introducing home-grown solutions to community issues.

In 1985, Obama was hired in Chicago as director of the Developing Communities Project (DCP) on Chicago's far South Side and worked there as a community organizer through May of 1988. During his term as Director, DCP had grown from a staff of one to thirteen and introduced a job training program, a college preparatory tutoring program, and a tenants' rights organization in Altgeld Gardens to confront the issues of unemployment, educational deficiencies, and disparities in residential rights.[160] In order to become a better civic servant, he entered Harvard Law School in 1988 to pursue higher education in the legal arena. While at Harvard, he became editor of the Harvard Law Review at the end of his first year

159 Ibid, p.159-162
160 Ibid, p.169

and was elevated to president of the journal in his second year. During his summers, he returned to Chicago to continue his labors in the civic arena. He worked as a summer associate at the law firms of Sidley Austin in 1989 and Hopkins & Sutter in 1990. After graduating with a Juris Doctor (J.D.) magna cum laude from Harvard in 1991, he not only returned to Chicago and accepted a two-year position as Visiting Law and Government Fellow at the University of Chicago Law School but also served as director for Project Vote, successor to the Southside Voter Registration Drive. His efforts on both fronts provided evidence that he possessed superior multi-tasking abilities and a high degree of commitment to the tasks in which he believed.[161]

Obama's civic participation grew in conjunction with his elevation in the educational areana. He was elevated to Professor at the University of Chicago Law School and taught constitutional law through 2004. He first served as Lecturer in 1992 and was, subsequently, elevated to Senior Lecturer in 1996.[162] While teaching constitutional law, he registered over 250,000 new voters as director of Project Vote in 1992 and served as an associate at Davis, Miner, Barnhill & Galland from 1993 to 1996 specializing in civil rights litigation and neighborhood economic development. He was elevated to Counsel of the law firm in 1996 to 2004. In addition, he served on the boards of directors for the Woods Fund of Chicago which worked to increase opportunities for the disadvantaged, the Joyce Foundation

---

161 Educational Britannica Educational. Black American Biographies: The Journey of
    Achievement. The Rosen Publishing Group, 2010, p.83
162 Ibid, p.83

which addressed environmental concerns and the Chicago Annenberg Challenge, which he founded in 1995, to promote higher education within the Chicago Public School System.[163]

These efforts, in essence, defined the base of the Obama Mission which appeared to focus on the improvement of the quality of life for the disadvantaged and the protection of civil rights under the laws of the land. His success in these areas and expertise as a law professor served as the source of Obama's civic foundation and became the springboard from which he launched his efforts in the political domain. By virtue of these accomplishments, Obama sought to succeed Illinois State Senator Alice Palmer and gained election to the Illinois State Senate in 1996.[164]

As an Illinois State Senator, Obama placed major a focus on the implementation of reform initiatives, particularly, in the arenas of ethics and health care. His 1997 efforts with Emil Jones Sr. and Judge Abner Mikva led to campaign finance reform which required disclosure of campaign finances deterring personal use of campaign funds. He supported legislation to increase child care coverage for families in need. Despite heavy opposition from police organizations, he supported and gained passage for legislation which required mandatory taping of interrogations to combat allegations of forced confessions by police officials.[165] These successes, which were accomplished through bi-partisan partnerships, impacted a wide range

---

163 Corsi, Jerome R. The Obama nation: leftist politics and the cult of personality. Simon and Schuster, 2008, p.137-138
164 Ibid, p.145
165 Slevin, Peter. Obama Forged Political Mettle In Illinois Capitol. The Washington Post, February 9, 2007

of citizens from the grass-roots Joe to political monarchs who appeared to be untouchable. Leveraging this wave, he was inspired to make his first attempt at a national political office and set his eyes on the United States Representative seat held by Congressman Bobby Rush.

Rush, who had been elected to the Chicago City Council in 1983, was also one who had been inspired by Harold Washington's example. Rush was one of Washington's largest supporters during the period known as Chicago's City Council Wars and he leveraged this kinship to earn election as United States Representative in 1993. His failed attempt against incumbent Mayor Richard M. Daley in 1999 for the office of Mayor for the City of Chicago, prompted Obama and several others to believe that he had lost the support of the African American community. With this assertion in mind, Obama challenged Rush during the Democratic primary in 2000 but lost the bid.[166]

Despite the loss, Obama resumed his focus on reform at the state level. He sponsored legislation to increase tax credits for low-income workers and promoted increased subsidies for childcare. In 2001, as co-chairman of the bipartisan Joint Committee on Administrative Rules, he supported payday loans regulations and predatory mortgage lending regulations aimed at averting home foreclosures. As the chairman of the Illinois Senate's Health and Human Services Committee in 2003, he sponsored legislation to monitor racial profiling requiring police to record the race of drivers they detained.[167] This legislation made Illinois the first state to mandate

---

166 Ibid. p.5
167 Ahn, Young Sop. How Obama Made It? Xlibris Corporation, 2009, p.62-63

videotaping of homicide interrogations.[168] With these successes, Obama's prominence had grown to a national scale due, in a large part, to his ability to reach across the political aisles to accomplish tough goals. Bolstering a strong record of successes, he made the leap to contend for a higher national office, namely, the United States Senate seat of Senator Peter Fitzgerald in 2003.

Incumbent Senator Peter Fitzgerald, who defeated former Harold Washington lieutenant Senator Carole Moseley-Braun during the prior term, had declined to run for his United States Senate seat citing personal reasons. Moseley-Braun had also declined to run for the seat as she sought the Democratic nod for the presidency of the United States of America. As such, Obama seized the opportunity and mounted his campaign for the United States Senate seat for the State of Illinois. On the campaign trail, Obama immediately opposed President George W. Bush's invasion of Iraq as proposed in 2002 and led multiple anti-war rallies in Illinois to publicly clarify his stance on the war. In doing so, he cemented himself as the front runner for the Senate seat over Republican candidate Jack Ryan who, due to personal reasons had withdrawn from the race. In order to field a viable challenger, the Republican Party scrambled to find candidates that would best represent their ideals. The search resulted with Alan Keyes as the Republican nominee and, after multiple verbal sparring matches, Obama won the election with over 70% of the vote in June of 2004.[169]

As a result of the wave of the success, Obama was tapped to give

168 Ibid, p.62
169 Ibid, p.63

the keynote address at the Democratic National Convention in July of 2004. It was during this speech that he was exposed to an international audience via multiple forms of media. In doing so he proved to be an oratorical master which boosted his level of prominence to a degree experienced by few African Americans before him.[170] With a focus on national unity, his words provided hope to millions and exuded a great sense of authenticity that made him appear magnanimous before America and the world and introduced him as a leader for change.

Sworn in as United States Senator in January 2005 as the lone Senate member of the Congressional Black Caucus, Obama's level of activity was extraordinary. He co-sponsored several Bills and Acts as a freshman senator on a bipartisan basis including the Secure America and Orderly Immigration and the Lugar-Obama Acts which were designed to improve the security of the nation. The 2006 Coburn–Obama Transparency Act authorized the establishment of USAspending.gov to provide transparency in federal spending. His diverse background was leveraged on the Foreign Relations, Environment and Public Works, and Veterans Affairs committees where he sponsored, introduced or supported legislation to provide aid to foreign countries, responsibility in the environmental protection and aid to families of veterans serving during wartime. He also served on the Health, Education, Labor and Pensions and Homeland Security and Governmental Affairs committees. He was the primary sponsor of the Democratic Republic of the Congo Relief, Security, and

---

170 Ibid, p.68-69

Democracy Promotion Act signed into law by President Bush in 2006. He sponsored a Senate amendment to the State Children's Health Insurance Program providing one year of job protection for family members caring for soldiers with combat-related injuries. He sponsored an amendment to the Defense Authorization Act adding safeguards for personality disorder military discharges in 2007 and sponsored the Iran Sanctions Enabling Act supporting divestment of state pension funds from Iran's oil and gas industry.[171] As many of these acts and bills received bipartisan support, these efforts by the freshman senator were tremendous and wreaked of a political savvy displayed by only the most seasoned politicians. The manner in which they were achieved cemented him as a unifying force and virtually eliminated the perception of him as a neophyte. By the light of these accomplishments and to the surprise of many, he announced his intent to seek the Democratic nomination for the office of President of the United States of America.

In front of the Old State Capitol building in Springfield, Illinois on February 10, 2007 from the stage of the Great Emancipator, Abraham Lincoln, Obama announced that it "was here, in Springfield, where North, South, East and West come together that I was reminded of the essential decency of the American people — where I came to believe that through this decency, we can build a more hopeful America. And that is why, in the shadow of the Old State Capitol, where Lincoln once called on a house divided to stand together, where common hopes and common dreams still live, I stand before

---

171 Ibid, p.76-77

you today to announce my candidacy for President of the United States of America."[172] Seven score years ago, the thought of the Democratic Party nominating an African American for any political office was unheard of. With the stronghold of the party in the southern states in the 1860s, there was the fear that the south would transform into a black man's world filled with disdain for southern whites. The fear also extended to the north and was exacerbated to the extent that the Democratic organizations of the States of Indiana and Pennsylvania moved to denounce negro suffrage in 1865 and 1866. Presidential candidate Samuel J. Tilden was even heard at the 1868 Democratic National Convention (DNC) in Albany, New York denouncing the veracity and intelligence of the negro.[173] However, four score and ten years later in 1958, Senator Jacob Javits of New York predicted that "speculation based on realistic appraisal of the fact for the march of progress and world events make it quite possible that a member of the Negro race will be appointed to a top cabinet post or elected to the Presidency or Vice Presidency by the year 2000."[174] In May of 1961, Robert Kennedy, reiterated a similar thought as he felt "that in the next 30 or 40 years, a Negro can also achieve the same position that my brother has as President of the United States, certainly within that period of time."[175] Martin Luther King, Jr., believed in 1964 as he iterated "I think we may be able to get a Negro President in less than 40 years."[176] The stride taken by

172 Kennedy-Shaffer, Alan. The Obama Revolution. Phoenix Books, Inc., 2009, p.166
173 Wood, Forrest G. Black Scare: The Racist Response to Emancipation and
    Reconstruction. University of California Press, 1970, p.117-118
174 Esquire, Volume 50, Esquire, Inc., 1958, p.236
175 Kennedy, Robert F. America the Beautiful. Putnam, 1969, p.52
176 Martin Luther King Jr., BBC interview, 1964

Channing Phillips four years thereafter to seek the Democratic nod was a viable attempt to make King's prediction a reality sooner rather than later. Within two score years of Phillips' run for the nod in 1968, the dream had come closer than ever before..

The Democratic field for the 2008 Presidential election included a number of political powerhouses and produced one of the most hotly contested races for the Democratic nomination in American history. In addition to Obama, the initial field included Senator Hillary Rodham Clinton of New York, former Senator John Edwards, Honorable Governor Bill Richardson of New Mexico, Representative Dennis Kucinich of Ohio, Senator Joe Biden of Delaware and other formidable candidates who had maintained stellar civic and political reputations. The field of Republican candidates included former Governors Mike Huckabee of Arkansas and Mitt Romney of Massachusetts; Senators Fred Thompson, John McCain and Ron Paul; Mayor Rudy Giuliani of New York City and a host of others.[177] From the onset, the candidates from both parties boldly presented their respective agendas through multiple media outlets but the first turn in the races came in January 2008 with the Iowa Caucuses.

Since 1972, the Iowa caucuses have been the first major electoral event for the Presidential nomination process and have, historically, served as a measurement tool to determine the candidates who would be more likely to win the nomination of their political party at that party's national convention.[178] As such, the Iowa Caucuses typically

177 Redlawsk, David P., Caroline J. Tolbert, Todd Donovan. Why Iowa?: How Caucuses and Sequential Elections Improve the Presidential Nominating Process. University of Chicago Press, 2010, p.4-5
178 Ibid, p.219

receive a high degree of national attention during presidential election years. At the start of the 2008 Iowa Caucuses, most polls had Clinton and Romney as the front-runners for the Democratic and Republican parties.

The wife of former President William Jefferson Clinton, Hillary Rodham Clinton brought a unique perspective to the table. She was the only candidate with first hand knowledge of presidential affairs and, as a former First Lady and the lone woman in the Democratic race, she garnered support from women of all races from across America. Her experience in the political arena extended back to 1974 with her service as Legal Counsel for the House Judiciary Committee. The quality of service in this role and those which succeeded made her a natural selection as Chairman of the Legal Services Corporation, a non-profit bipartisan organization established by United States Congress, from 1977 to 1982 under the administrations of Presidents Jimmy Carter and Ronald Reagan.[179] Her efforts in the private sector in the 1980s were of such a high caliber that she was named one of the hundred most influential attorneys by the National Law Journal in 1988 and 1991.[180] These experiences coupled, arguably, made her one of the most formidable candidates in history.

The former Chief Executive Officer of Bain & Company, co-founder of Bain Capital and leader within The Church of Jesus Christ of Latter-Day Saints, Mitt Romney's experience in the business arena and polished image were the primary factors which contributed to his

---

179 Ford, Lynne E. Encyclopedia of Women and American Politics. Infobase Publishing, 2008, p.119
180 Schwartz, Richard Alan. The 1990s. Infobase Publishing, 2006, p.414

rise in the Republican ranks at the turn of the 21ˢᵗ Century. Hired by Bain & Company in 1977, Romney had risen through the ranks of the management consulting firm leveraging his high confidence and intellect to become a Vice President of the company by 1978. He quickly became one of the company's best consultants which prompted Bill Bain to offer him an opportunity to head Bain Capital, a private equity investment firm, in the 1980s. From 1984 through the 1990s, his efforts contributed to massive profits earned by Bain Capital, however, with Bain & Company on the brink of bankruptcy in the early 1990s, he returned home to steer the helm of the sinking ship.[181] Through creativity and superior talent management, he effectively, transformed the company into a multi-million dollar private equity firm. With Juris Doctorate and Masters in Business Administration degrees from Harvard, he leveraged data analysis through strategic audits to produce an accurate picture of the company's current state and manged his resources to implement solutions which turn the company around.[182] As his success at Bain & Company and Bain Capital had provided him with regular appearances in the Boston area periodicals, he mounted an attempt for the Massachusetts United States Senate seat as a Republican in 1994 against incumbent Democratic Senator Ted Kennedy. After the loss, he returned to Bain Capital until he was tapped to lead the 2002 Salt Lake City Olympic Committee in 1999.[183] Riding the success of the

181 Swidey, Neil; Ebbert, Stephanie. Romney Determined to Make Mark Early. Deseret Morning News, July 4, 2007
182 Hewitt, Hugh. A Mormon in the White House? 10 Things Every American Should Know About Mitt Romney. Regnery Publishing, 2007, p.52
183 Williams, Wendy, Robert Whitcomb. Cape Wind: Money, Celebrity, Class, Politics, and the Battle for Our Energy Future: Easyread Large Edition. ReadHowYouWant.com,

Olympic Winter Games, Romney re-rentered the political arena as a candidate for the gubernatorial race for the State of Massachusetts. In November of 2002, Romney won the race convincingly and became the 70th Governor of Massachusetts.[184]

While Clinton and Romney both presented impressive credentials, they were not selected by the voters at the 2008 Iowa Caucuses. Of the Democratic field, Clinton placed third behind Obama and John Edwards. Through the succeeding months, Obama continued to expand his audience which was receptive to his messages of change and hope. Like Dr. Martin Luther King Jr., his method of delivery flowed with the vocal tones and rhythm of an African American Baptist Preacher. Leveraging his multi-cultural background, civic achievements and educational experiences, he had a wide appeal but the heated debates with Clinton eventually polarized the Democratic party. Many seemed torn to select either an African American male or an experienced white female for the nominee. Despite the battles, Obama's success at Iowa carried him through the remaining races which translated into a multitude of pledged delegate votes. By June Obama had gained the edge in pledged delegate counts and secured his status as the frontrunner going into the DNC in August of 2008.[185]

Huckabee, a former Arkansas Governor and preacher, had also pitched an upset at the 2008 Iowa Caucuses as he outgained Romney for the majority of the Iowa Republican caucus votes. While he

2009, p.308

184 Carr, Howie. The brothers Bulger: how they terrorized and corrupted Boston for a quarter century. Hachette Digital, Inc., 2006

185 Redlawsk, David P., Caroline J. Tolbert, Todd Donovan. Why Iowa?: How Caucuses and Sequential Elections Improve the Presidential Nominating Process. University of Chicago Press, 2010, p.20

outflanked his Republican foes in Iowa, Huckabee had lost the ground gained within a month of the caucuses to Senator John McCain..[186] McCain, who had positioned himself as a "Maverick", touted his experience and independent judgment to rise through the polls. By February, he had surpassed both Huckabee and Romney and, by March, gained the majority of the Republican pledged delegates.[187] These victories secured his status as the frontrunner going into the September Republican National Convention (RNC).

On Monday, August 25, 2008 in Denver, Colorado, the DNC opened with an attendance that nearly doubled the counts from four years prior. The hope and anticipation of a grand historical moment filled the air with the likelihood of the selection of the first African American by a major American political party as the nominee for the highest office in the land. As the delegate votes were counted, the voice of Hillary Rodham Clinton emerged from among them conceding her support to Obama as the nominee. The final tally transformed the hope of millions of African Americans over the globe to a reality as the DNC announced Obama as the Democratic nominee for the President of the United States of America. With his running mate, Senator Joe Biden, firmly in his corner, Obama accepted the presidential nomination on Thursday, August 28, 2008., the forty-fifth anniversary of Dr. King's "I Have a Dream" speech, becoming the first African American presidential nominee of a major poitical party.[188] Within one week of Obama's acceptance, Senator John

---

186 Skipper, John C. The Iowa caucuses: first tests of presidential aspiration, 1972-2008. McFarland, 2010, p.150
187 Ibid, 2010, p.20
188 Clayon, Dewey M. The Presidential Campaign of Barack Obama: A Critical Analysis

McCain along with his running mate, Alaska Governor Sarah Palin, accepted the nomination for the Republican National Convention. With the Third Party candidates identified and prepared to contend, the race for the White House was set for the general election.

November 4, 2008, "Super Tuesday", found over 131 million votes cast and yielded a clear winner with the following results: [189]

Candidate	Party	Popular Vote	Electoral Vote
Barack H. Obama	Democrat	69,456,897	365
John McCain	Republican	59,934,814	173
Ralph Nader	Independent	738,475	0
Bob Barr	Libertarian	523,686	0
Chuck Baldwin	Constitution	199,314	0
Cynthia McKinney	Green	161,603	0
Other		242,539	0
Total		131,257,328	538

After obtaining nearly 68% of the electoral vote, the Honorable Barack H. Obama became the first African American to be elected President of the United States of America.

Indeed, change had come to America as the face of her new leader had a darker tone than all of the others who had come before him. The victory had certainly satisfied the hopes of millions stirring up such strong emotions that they were emitted uncontrollably by young and seasoned alike. In an interview with renown poet, Maya Angelou by Harry Smith of CBS News, she exclaimed "I'm so proud and filled, I

of a Racially Transcendent Strategy. Taylor & Francis, 2010, p.121
189 Bunch, Will. The Backlash: Right-Wing Radicals, High-Def Hucksters, and Paranoid Politics in the Age of Obama. Harper Collins, 2010, p.31

can hardly talk without weeping." Her emotions were echoed at the start of the poem she issued for the inaugaration in which she states "Out of the huts of history's shame I rise up from a past rooted in pain....I rise. Bringing the hopes that my ancestors gave, I am the hope and the dream of the slave." Jesse Jackson, who wept tears of joy at Obama's inauguration noted with great anticipation that "he hadn't gotten much sleep for the past two nights, because it was almost like 1862, December 31, you knew the next day the Emancipation Proclamation would be signed and people couldn't sleep."[190] In his tears were precious memories of how his father, who fought the Nazis in World War II, came back home and had no rights. His tears focused, also, on the martyrs of the civil rights movement, on the pride they would have felt to see a portion of the change they fought for materialize. "It's been a long time coming", stated Obama at his Victory Speech in Chicago's Grant Park, "but tonight, because of what we did on this day, in this election at this defining moment, change has come to America."[191]

---

190 ABC's Good Morning America, broadcast November 5, 2008
191 Cohen, David Elliot, Mark Greenberg, Howard Dodson. Obama: The Historic Front
    Pages. Sterling Publishing Company, Inc., 2009, p.95

Epilogue

"Never let go of hope. One day you will see that it all

has finally come together." - Anonymous

"Frederick Douglass articulated to the Commemorative meeting of the 23rd Anniversary of Emancipation in the District of Columbia in 1885 that "it is the soul that makes a nation great or small, noble or ignoble, weak or strong". He further declared that "it is the soul that exalts it to happiness or sinks it into misery...the spiritual side of humanity. Though occult and impalpable, it is as real as iron. The laws of its life are spiritual, not carnal, and it must conform to these laws or it starves and dies." The substance of the soul of the United States of America lay in her Preamble to her Constitution which states:

> "We the People of the United States, in Order to form a more perfect Union, establish Justice, insure domestic Tranquility, provide for the common defense, promote the general Welfare, and secure the Blessings of Liberty to ourselves and our Posterity, do ordain and establish this Constitution for the United States of America."

At the time of its writing, these words, although eloquent and moving, were not equally enforced for all Americans and the resulting inequities became a cancer which threatened America's very soul. However, it was through the constant battles and by the blood, sweat and tears of those who truly believed in liberty, that the line of sight into those solemn words had begun to gain some credibility for African Americans.

Nearly a century after the passage of the 13th and 14th

amendments, the Civil Rights legislation passed by the nation provided evidence to the fact that the discriminatory practices had not died or faded away. Many Americans felt that the latter would be the balm to finally heal the scars of racism. Unfortunately her cancerous sting still survived which required continued vigilance to combat her demands. Through these struggles, ground was gained within the local and national political ranks and it was this ground gained in conjunction with civil rights victories that an environment within which African American could thrive was achieved.

Activist and comedian, Dick Gregory, was asked overseas, if he felt that the election of Obama had been the point of the struggle."That would have been an insult," Gregory said. "We weren't out there, black folks and white folks, going to jail and getting killed, for a black president. We were out there fighting for the least amongst us to have the right to vote. Out of that came a black president." While Jesse Jackson noted that "this young man (Obama) who has done such a marvelous job, who in some sense mobilized the consciousness of the world" he also admonished that, relative to racial relations, "we're learning to embrace....but there is still 'unfinished business' in poverty-stricken urban ghettos and barrios." Jackson also affirmed that Obama's promises to reinvest in America mean that "the substance is very connected with the hope" which implies that the age-old responsibility to represent those who are under-represented remains a major focus for citizens of African descent and others who struggle by virtue of the tone of their skin.

Overall, the labor to complete the unfinished business is the substance that African Americans hoped for with the selection of Obama to the highest office of the land and it is this responsibility as engaged by his predecessors that has now been placed on his lap to carry.

As Douglass concluded a portion of his speech to the citizens of the District of Columbia he further admonished that "the life of the nation is secure only while the nation is honest, truthful and virtuous, for upon these conditions depends the life of its life." (The Mind and Heart of Frederick Douglass adapted by Barbara Ritchie, Crowell, 1968, page 194-195)

The bruises

Well, the hope which was personified in Obama is not the end game. It is only the beginning – a beginning to a new future of symmettry and mutli-cultural success in which all people are included in the "We" listed in the Preamble.

Index

Griffin, Charles	27
Griffin T. Watson Lodge	8
Gross, John J.	12
GUOOF	17p.
Hamburgers	25
Hancock, Richard M.	12
Harvard	80, 89p., 99
Harvard Law Review	89
Harvard Law School	89
Harvey, William	41
Hatcher, Richard	64
Hayes, Charles Arthur	55, 62
Hopkins & Sutter	90
Huckabee, Mike	97, 100p.
Hudlun, Joseph	12
Human Rights Act	54
Humphrey, Hubert	71p., 74
Hussein, Saddam	77
Hyde, Henry	58
Illinois and Michigan Canal	3
Illinois Commerce Commission	27
Illinois Equal Rights League	15
Illinois General Assembly	13, 15, 27
Iowa Caucuses	83, 97p., 100
Iran Sanctions Enabling Act	95
Isbell, Louis	8
Jackson, Jesse	59p.,64p.,75pp.,83,88,103,75
James, Daniel 'Chappie'	32

Occidental College	87p.
Oglesby, Richard	9
Omega Psi Phi	44
Operation PUSH	60
Oriental Lodge	21
Orr, David	61
Owen, Chandler	28, 34
Palin, Sarah	102
Palmer, Alice	91
Partee, Cecil	52p.
Paul, Ron	97
Payne, William C.	69
Phillips, Channing	65, 72p., 97
Prince Hall Mason	8,11p.,29,40,42p.,47,61
Project Vote	90
Provident Hospital, Hospital	17
Punahou School	87
Quinn Chapel	6p., 44
Ragen Colts	25
Rangel, Charles	83
Rayner, A.A.	48
Reagan, Ronald	58, 98
Reeb, James J.	53
Republican National Convention	67, 79
Richardson, Bill	4, 97
Richardson, H.H.	4
Richardson, Mary	4
Rizzo, Frank L.	59

RNC	67, 101
Robinson, Renault	52
Romney, Mitt	97pp.
Roosevelt, Theodore	69
Rush, Bobby	60p.,78,82,92
Russell, Al	24
Ryan, Jack	93
Sabath, Joseph	26
Salina Normal School	21
Salt Lake City Olympic Committee	99
Saunders, William	26
Sawyer, Eugene	60p.
School Improvement Act	62
Scott, William T.	69
Seale, Bobby	46
Sengstacke, John	43
Sharpton, Al	80, 82p.
Sidley Austin	90
Simon, Paul M.	82
Slavery	3,8p.,12,14,65p.,68
Smith, Al	74
Smith, George	12
Southside Voter Registration	88, 90
State of Illinois v. Tonson	26
Stewart, Bennet McVey	48
Summer Guards	12
Taylor, George Edwin	69
Taylor, Jim	57
The Conservator	16, 18

CPSIA information can be obtained
at www.ICGtesting.com
Printed in the USA
BVHW012321020822
643676BV00002B/8